ROLL FOR SANDWICH
COOKBOOK

FOR GAMING ENTHUSIASTS AND ADVENTUROUS EATERS

Dedication

To my wife, Audrey, and my daughters for believing in me and tolerating piles of condiments in our home.

© 2025 by Jacob A. Pauwels and Fox Chapel Publishing Company, Inc.

Roll for Sandwich® Cookbook for Gaming Enthusiasts and Adventurous Eaters is an original work, first published in 2025 by Fox Chapel Publishing Company, Inc. All rights reserved. No part of this publication may be reproduced, stored in a retrieval system or transmitted, in any form or by any means, electronic, mechanical, photocopying, recording or otherwise, without the prior written permission of the copyright holders.

Roll for Sandwich® is a registered trademark of Jacob Pauwels.

Unless otherwise noted, photos are copyright Jacob Pauwels.

The following photos are from Shutterstock.com: cover border: Vasya Kobelev; cover background: Mo.Artist; cover and 3 leather texture: Dmitr1ch; cover and 2 dice: fvgromanelli; ends (combined/modified): Foontntd and Alexandr III; page texture throughout: Lukasz Szwaj; 3 background: Dariusz Matuszek; parchment 10, 54, 70, 92, 120: Andrey_Kuzmin; backgrounds 10–11, 36–37, 54–55, 70–71, 92–93, 120–121: n_defender; 133: Esther H. Derksen; dice icons 134–139 (modified): Alexandr III

ISBN 978-1-4971-0541-6

Library of Congress Control Number: 2025936692

To learn more about the other great books from Fox Chapel Publishing, or to find a retailer near you, call toll-free at 800-457-9112 or visit us at www.FoxChapelPublishing.com.

We are always looking for talented authors.
To submit an idea, please send a brief inquiry to acquisitions@foxchapelpublishing.com.

Or write to:
Fox Chapel Publishing
903 Square Street
Mount Joy, PA 17552

Printed in China
First printing

FSC
www.fsc.org
MIX
Paper | Supporting responsible forestry
FSC® C193369

ROLL FOR SANDWICH

COOKBOOK

FOR GAMING ENTHUSIASTS AND ADVENTUROUS EATERS

GO ON A MEALTIME QUEST WITH
THE ROLL OF THE DICE!

JACOB A. PAUWELS

Fox Chapel
PUBLISHING

Contents

WELCOME TO YOUR NEXT CULINARY ADVENTURE   6

The Story of Roll for Sandwich   7

CRITICAL HITS   10

The 42   12
Ginger Dreams   14
The Jurassic Pork   16
Risk It for the Brisket   18
The Merle   20
The Demi Delhi-catessen   22
The Crunch Squad   24
The Cheese Blessing   26
The Rotten Soldier   28
Pure Dead Brilliant   30
The Peppadew® Pig   32
The Slawful Good   34

THE CUSP OF GREATNESS   36

The Comfortably Numb   38
The Toast Balone-y   40
Sandwich a la King   42
Curd to the Wise   44
Dim Sum Pair-O-Dice   46
The Swiss Near Miss   48
The Elephant in the Room   50
Taste of the Wild   52

FESTIVAL OF SEASONS   54

The Heart Attack   56
Sweet Summer Pie   58
The Cold Day in Shell   60
The PureBREAD   62
How the Nog Stoll Christmas   64
The Nightmare Before Christmas   66
The H.O.A.   68

Epic Failures — 70

The Failed Stealth Check	72
The Abomination	74
The Crabomination	76
All Taffy, No Laughy	78
The Nasty Patty	80
Beanhamut	82
Deck the Halls	84
The Bad Buddy	86
The Descent Into Avernus	88
I'm Only Cumin	90

Curiosities — 92

The Beginning	94
The Za-mbie	96
Sandwichception	98
The Fetch Quest	100
Tom	102
The Frozen Pizza	104
The Brittle Lily	106
The Beverly Hillbilly	108
The Shadow of a Trout	110
Chopped & Screwed	112
Cretaceous Cookie Crumble	114
The Ferryman's Fee	116
The Pickle Priest	118

Undiscovered Treasures — 120

The Roc Salad Wrap	122
The P.B.P.	124
The Bologna Buzz	126
The Strawberry Fairy	128
The Goodberry	130

Your Own Adventure: Roll for Sandwich at Home — 132

How to Roll for Sandwich	132
Choosing Items for the Roll Sheets	132
Sourcing Interesting Ingredients	133
Roll Sheets	134

FAQs	140
Index	142
About the Author	144

Welcome to Your Next Culinary Adventure

There's a good chance you know all about Roll for Sandwich (RFS), the video series I started in 2022, in which I let a roll of the dice determine my lunch. It blends elements from the tabletop roleplaying games I love (think Dungeons & Dragons®) with my excitement for food creation and exploration. I roll dice to choose my bread, my main ingredients, and all the sauces and extras. And every sandwich I make, appetizing or not, I eat and rate for the viewers.

This book is a record of many of those lunches. In the following pages, you'll join me on a food-fueled journey through ingredients and combinations from tried-and-true to squarely outside the comfort zone. I've long had requests for a Roll for Sandwich cookbook from my community of enthusiasts, and I'm excited to finally make it a reality.

I've broken the sandwiches into sections from the absolute winners (Critical Hits), to almost-there creations (those on the Cusp of Greatness), to clear misses (Epic Failures). I've also included special seasonal standouts (Festival of Seasons), the most memorable creations (Curiosities), and even a few new, exclusive combinations just for you (Undiscovered Treasures). I relive my first taste of each from the episode, share my rating, and show you exactly how to replicate the experiment so you can rate each one at home!

Finally, this book wouldn't be complete if I didn't help you get started with your own epic food adventure. I've included sheets you can use to customize the game for your own meals based on the ingredients in your own fridge. Make any lunch or picnic a bold quest into the unknown. Will you discover a new favorite sandwich? Or brave one of the unimaginable horrors birthed by the dark whims of the dice? Or maybe even create your own brand-new combination never before seen in sandwich history? Your story remains to be told, Adventurer. Grab your dice, and let's roll!

THE STORY OF ROLL FOR SANDWICH

Hi, I'm Jake! I've been telling stories my whole life. My storytelling has taken many different forms over the years; from running around in the backyard "slaying monsters" with a stick, to making videos in high school and college, to writing and performing music, to playing in and running fantasy roleplaying games with friends to, well, *sandwiches*.

Roll For Sandwich began on TikTok in April of 2022. I joined the app back in 2020 as a means of staying connected and had no real plan to create content. I truly enjoyed that "silly little video app" as just a means of entertainment and connection. When it became easier to gather with friends in person again, I started playing Dungeons & Dragons more often. When a friend of mine was unable to continue as dungeon master (DM), I knew it was finally time for me to try my hand at DMing! I decided to make a *new* TikTok account to document the experiment. The setting I'd chosen for my small group of friends was the world of the novel I had been writing at the time, Aardia—so, logically, I called my channel "Adventures in Aardia."

In those early days, I posted videos related to my campaign and began building a small community of followers, mostly within the roleplaying community. At the time, I was a stay-at-home dad, so most of my day-to-day consisted of taking care of my then-toddler. I was having fun posting to TikTok and making content. I have a degree in television production that I never really got to take full advantage of, so it was fun to use my skills and creativity to talk about my passions and interests. I expected the small audience I was developing on TikTok would be the extent of it.

One day, while feeding my child lunch, I had the idea for Roll for Sandwich. I had just gone grocery shopping, and my fridge was fully stocked, so I decided to take a chance and randomize my lunch! Watching that first video now, it's easy to tell that I didn't expect much from it, but there are inklings of what the show would become. Even at the start, I planned to make Roll for Sandwich a series, but I had no idea how incredibly successful it would become. It gained immediate traction in a way that I never could have anticipated.

After watching my following grow to almost 50K overnight, I immediately made another episode. I didn't put a ton of effort into the first few videos, but people truly adored the concept, and it took off like wildfire! That initial bump of engagement was all I needed to fully commit to Roll for Sandwich.

WHY SANDWICHES?

People often ask me why I picked sandwiches. There are many foods and beverages to which you can apply the randomized recipe formula (and since I began my journey, many other creators have done just that). For me, though, it could only ever have been sandwiches. I have loved sandwiches since I was a little kid carrying my paper-sack lunches to school. They were one of the first foods I learned to prepare myself, and even as an adult, completely outside of my obligations to the show, I eat sandwiches frequently.

Sandwiches seem to follow a formula: Bread, meat, cheese, vegetable, sauce—these basic categories form our idea of a "sandwich." Yet some of the most famous sandwiches break the mold. A peanut butter and jelly is just two spreads between two slices of bread, but it's one of the most beloved sandwiches in the country. There are hot debates about what officially qualifies as a sandwich (I'm on team "a hot dog is a sandwich" forever).

And there's the beauty—sandwiches are infinitely versatile. They can be hot or cold, sweet or savory, meat-heavy or meat-free, filling or light—"sandwiches" is a broad genre of food. They exist in one form or another in just about every culture on earth (and probably beyond). There are always new combinations to try—especially when you let the dice free you from the shackles of convention. The combination of the general formula with the versatility provides both a comfortable familiarity for the audience and a fun system of rules to buck against.

And that's why Roll for *Sandwich* was always fated to be.

A sandwich is just a sandwich . . . until it isn't! Earl the sandwich mimic is a great sidekick.

Since then, I've poured a ton of time and talent into the series, constantly pushing to improve it, and have been having a blast doing so! I've had so many amazing opportunities come my way, including collaborations with the Detroit Lions, the McElroy brothers, Dimension 20, the 2023 Dungeons & Dragons movie, and so many others. Now I'm finally publishing the cookbook that everyone has been asking for since those early days!

Making Roll for Sandwich is the best job I've ever had, and I'm so thankful for everyone, including you reading this right now, for supporting me through the process. It's made even the most heinous of sandwiches worth it!

RESPECTING FOOD

An integral part of Roll for Sandwich is advocating against food waste and respecting food as a finite resource. There is an unfortunate trend toward food waste in the online spaces occupied by shows like Roll for Sandwich. Some content creators rely on the shock factor to drum up views—making purposefully gross recipes or recipes featuring an outlandish amount of food. They use the food for a single video and then often discard it—food used for clicks, views, and clout, then thrown into a landfill.

Modern food production requires a lot of resources. It takes around 240 gallons (910L) of water to produce one loaf of bread, for example. And water is not the only resource it takes to produce food. Labor, fossil fuels, equipment, and more all go into the production of our food. To purchase food with the intent to throw it away is disrespectful not only to the people who work hard to grow, produce, harvest, and transport our food, it's also disrespectful to those who are food insecure. According to the US Department of Agriculture, almost 13 percent of American households (approximately 17 million total) were food insecure in 2022. Meanwhile, some online creators are throwing away pounds of food every week.

Even though I've used my platform to make my lunch into a game, this is an issue I don't take lightly. I have worked hard to make it clear that I am very serious about respecting food and the value it has as a resource in our lives. That is one of the main reasons why the rules of Roll for Sandwich have always included this: *The entire sandwich, good or bad, gets eaten.* I hope that when you try Roll for Sandwich at home, you'll keep this rule in mind. And I hope you always have food on your plate.

My 2022 collaboration with the Detroit Lions.

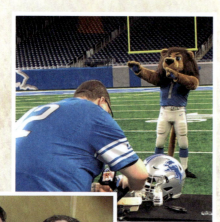

With Luke Gygax, son of D&D creator Gary Gygax, at Gen Con 2024.

With actress Sophia Lillis (Doric) at the 2023 *Dungeons & Dragons: Honor Among Thieves* movie press junket.

With Jim Behymer of Sandwich Tribunal (@sandwichtribunal) in 2024.

On Fox17 local news channel in 2024.

Filming "A Sandwich with Sea Turtles" at Sea Life Michigan in 2023.

Tabletop Terminology

Though my channel started within the tabletop gaming sphere, my sandwich content quickly grew to encompass a much wider audience. It was then that I added to my classic intro phrase, "Good afternoon, D&D TikTok *and beyond*!" You might very well be among the "beyond," with little (to no) knowledge of tabletop roleplaying games. For those of you who found RFS through your love of sandwiches, the following is a helpful breakdown of some of the most common gaming terms you'll encounter while watching the show or reading this book. Knowledge of these terms and tabletop gaming in general is in no way required to enjoy Roll for Sandwich, but this overview should alleviate your curiosity.

Advantage/Disadvantage—"Rolling with advantage" means to roll two twenty-sided dice (D20s; see "D20, D6, etc.," below) and use the better result of the two. Conversely, "rolling with disadvantage" means rolling two D20s and using the worse result.

Cantrip—A cantrip is a low-powered spell. Cantrips are considered "spell level 0" and can be cast "at will," meaning they do not require the use of a spell slot (see "Spell Slot," below).

Crit/Critical Hit—A critical hit is when you roll so well on a D20 attack roll that your damage is doubled. This can occur in a few ways, with rolling the highest number on the die being the most common.

D&D—"D and D" refers to "Dungeons & Dragons®," one of the most popular tabletop roleplaying games. It has been around since the 1970s.

DM/GM—DM/GM stands for "dungeon master/game master," and refers to the person responsible for organizing and facilitating a tabletop roleplaying game.

D20, D6, etc.—D20 refers to a twenty-sided die, D6 refers to a six-sided die, and so on.

Mimic—A mimic is a fantasy creature that changes shape. It often takes the shape of inanimate objects, such as treasure chests, and waits for an unsuspecting adventurer to draw near. When the adventurer tries to open the chest, expecting treasure, the mimic ambushes them. Earl, the box I feed my naughty dice to, is a sandwich mimic.

Nat 20—A "Nat 20" or a "natural twenty" is when a twenty is rolled on a twenty-sided die. In many TTRPGs, a Nat 20 is considered an automatic success or a critical hit. The word "natural" refers to the fact that an actual 20 is shown on the die rather than your roll reaching a total of twenty by adding points from your character's skills, weapons, etc.

Spell Slot—A spell slot is a consumable resource that allows you to cast spells. Spell slots and spells have levels, and the level of the spell slot you use to cast a spell must be equal to or higher than the level of the spell. (For example, you can use a level 3 spell slot to cast a level 1, 2, or 3 spell, but the only spell you can cast with a level 1 spell slot is a level 1 spell.) Cantrips do not cost a spell slot.

TTRPG/RPG—These acronyms stand for "Tabletop Roleplaying Game" and "Roleplaying Game" respectively.

Critical Hits

A broken clock is right twice a day, given enough time a room full of monkeys with typewriters can reproduce the full works of Shakespeare, and, sometimes, the dice on Roll for Sandwich actually create a delicious sandwich! The following sandwiches are the cream of the RFS crop. Many of them have been tried and tasted by other sandwich influencers and have passed the test. If you make any sandwiches from this book, these are the ones to start with!

10/10

The 42

Episode 42 | **AIRDATE:** June 10, 2022 | **PREP TIME:** 5 minutes | **Makes one sandwich**

When I get asked which sandwiches have surprised me most, "The 42" is never far from my mind. Leaving your lunch up to chance almost always results in a strange combination, but when the dice create a sandwich that is both unexpected and surprisingly delicious, it feels like a true victory.

This sandwich seemed, on paper, to be doomed from the start. Rolling peanut butter as the main, then adding cheese, two vegetables, and a sauce was almost certainly not going to work, right? Well, thankfully, I got lucky—or perhaps I was blessed from the great beyond by the late, great Douglas Adams, whose comedic sci-fi series, The Hitchhiker's Guide to the Galaxy, I referenced several times throughout the episode.

The 42 ended up being a mix of flavors that invoked Thai cuisine: peanuts, spice, and even the familiar iceberg crunch of a lettuce wrap. The sandwich is rich and decadent, filled with creamy textures and a fair amount of fat. This sandwich was so surprising that it started a sort of tradition on Roll for Sandwich and "Sandwichtok"—other sandwich-based creators re-create my 10 out of 10 sandwiches and give their own reviews. The 42 achieved wide popularity as a surprisingly great sandwich—and I hope you enjoy trying your own version!

INGREDIENTS

- 2 slices Italian bread
- Crunchy peanut butter
- 1–1½ ounces spreadable goat cheese
- ½ small avocado, sliced
- 10 banana pepper rings
- 1–2 iceberg lettuce leaves
- Drizzle of KPOP Foods Kimchi Mayo, or a suitable alternative
- Drizzle of lime juice, optional

INSTRUCTIONS

1. Optional: If you prefer a firmer sandwich, begin by toasting both slices of Italian bread. Otherwise, start with step 2.

2. Spread a layer of peanut butter on one slice of bread. I used crunchy for my sandwich, but you can use creamy if you prefer.

3. Spread the goat cheese on the other slice of bread.

4. Add a layer of avocado to the peanut butter slice.

5. With a paper towel, pat dry the banana pepper rings. Add them in a single layer on top of the avocado.

6. Add the iceberg lettuce on top of the peppers, keeping the leaves as whole as possible.

7. On the other slice of bread, add a generous drizzle of the mayo on top of the goat cheese.

8. Optional: Drizzle a little lime juice over the lettuce.

9. Close the sandwich by adding the second slice of bread on top, goat cheese side down.

10. Cut the sandwich in half diagonally and enjoy!

The mix of crunchy peanut butter, goat cheese, avocado, banana peppers, lettuce, and kimchi mayo might sound odd on paper, but this sandwich has gained a lot of fans!

10/10

Ginger Dreams

Episode 51 | AIRDATE: August 1, 2022 | PREP TIME: 5 minutes | Makes one sandwich

In case you haven't figured it out yet, my favorite food is sandwiches! There are a few foods that come close to unseating the reigning bread-enclosed champ, and one of those (despite the fraught history of fish on RFS) is sushi. The Ginger Dreams was able to capture some of the sushi vibes I love and marry them with the flavors of an Italian cold-cut sandwich. It worked much better than I expected. The salami, Havarti cheese, and pickled onions have a tanginess to them that played very well when combined with the ginger. What made this sandwich shine, though, was the Japanese mayo.

Japanese mayo is made using egg yolks only, so it's creamier and more savory. It also usually contains MSG, giving it a nice punch of umami flavor. That creaminess combined with all the tangy and acidic elements was a match made in sandwich heaven.

This sandwich was also the first RFS sandwich to officially be named. When I started season 2, I introduced the practice of naming each sandwich after scoring. This one isn't my most creative name, I must admit, but it's a fair starting point. The Ginger Dreams persists as a sandwich worth replicating!

INGREDIENTS

- 2 slices Whole Grains Oatnut bread, or a suitable alternative
- Butter
- 3 large slices salami
- 2 slices Havarti
- ¼ cup pickled red onion
- ½ cup green pepper, cut into ⅜" (1cm) slices
- ¼ cup pickled ginger strips
- A healthy drizzle of Japanese mayo

INSTRUCTIONS

1. Place two untoasted slices of Oatnut bread onto a plate.

2. Butter the bread, being careful not to shred the untoasted bread. I recommend using room-temperature butter for this.

3. Layer the salami on one slice of bread.

4. On top of the salami, layer the slices of Havarti.

5. On top of the cheese, arrange the pickled onions in a single layer covering the whole sandwich. You want some in every bite!

6. Add the green pepper slices in a layer on top of the pickled onions.

7. Add the pickled ginger strips on top of the green pepper. You can use pink or white ginger, whichever you prefer—the taste will be the same.

8. On the other slice of bread, apply a healthy squirt of Japanese mayo.

9. Close the sandwich by adding the top slice of bread, mayo side down.

10. Cut the sandwich in half diagonally and enjoy!

Tip

If you have trouble finding pickled ginger, check your local Asian grocery store. You can also find Japanese mayo at Asian grocery stores, though it is becoming increasingly available in major grocery chains.

This sandwich is a perfect blend of the umami flavor and creaminess of Japanese mayo and the stronger bite of the pickled ingredients.

Ginger Dreams 15

10/10

The Jurassic Pork

Episode 81 | AIRDATE: October 12, 2022 | PREP TIME: 20 minutes | Makes one sandwich

This sandwich boasts Jurassic proportions of fried pork in three different forms, making it a savory salt-bomb in the best way. It would almost be too much without the combined saving grace of the banana peppers and the dill pickle mustard. Both bring a much-needed acid that cuts through the grease and fat of the fried meats with bright, tangy flavors.

The Jurassic Pork is not for the faint of heart, but it is one of the better examples of times when the dice seemed to stick to a coherent theme to create a very logical, if a bit extra, sandwich. If any sandwich could be a match for the dinosaurs, it would be this one: "meatier" than the rest!

INGREDIENTS

- 2 slices sprouted grain bread, toasted and buttered
- 4–6 ounces Spam®, cut into ⅜" (1cm) slices
- 2 slices bologna
- 2 slices Swiss cheese
- 2–4 leaves iceberg lettuce
- ¼ cup banana pepper rings
- 3 strips bacon
- A healthy drizzle of dill pickle mustard

INSTRUCTIONS

1. Pan fry the Spam slices until they are brown on both sides. Add the Spam in an even layer on top of one of the slices of bread.

2. Using the same pan, fry the bologna, browning the slices on both sides. Add the bologna on top of the spam.

3. Layer the Swiss cheese on top of the bologna.

4. Add an even layer of lettuce on top of the cheese.

5. Add an even layer of banana peppers.

6. Prepare the bacon using your preferred method. Add the prepared bacon on top of the banana peppers.

7. Spread a layer of dill pickle mustard on the buttered side of the other piece of bread.

8. Put the top piece of bread sauce side down on top of the sandwich.

9. Cut the sandwich in half diagonally and enjoy!

Tip

I prefer to use precooked bacon for sandwiches—it is quick and easy to prepare in small batches.

There could have been too much fried pork on this sandwich, but the banana peppers and dill pickle mustard kept the salt and grease in check.

10/10

Risk It for the Brisket

Episode 147 | AIRDATE: May 9, 2023 | PREP TIME: 5 minutes | Makes one sandwich

Risk It for the Brisket is one of the most normal, logically-put-together sandwiches to come out of the series to date. Unsurprisingly, it scored a 10/10, even though I was genuinely afraid I was tempting fate (the episode immediately before had also been a 10/10, the first time in show history).

I often still crave this sandwich! Warm, juicy beef brisket pairs perfectly with creamy Gournay cheese. The slight bite of the chives, shallots, and green onion goes great with the savory meat, while the shredded carrot adds great texture and a small amount of sweetness. The Dusseldorf mustard brings it all home with a splash of acidity that cuts through the richness of the beef and cheese. While lesser sandwiches on the show have fallen apart, the firm, hearty sourdough bread used here is the perfect vehicle to keep this one together.

This is just a great sandwich, plain and simple. Other 10/10 sandwiches in this book might be weird and quirky, but this one should be the easiest for the new initiate to digest!

INGREDIENTS

- 2 slices sourdough bread
- 6 ounces cooked beef brisket, pulled or shredded
- 3 ounces Gournay cheese with shallot and chive
- 1 green onion, sliced into ⅜" (1cm) or smaller rounds
- 1 medium carrot, shredded
- A sprinkle of dried dill weed
- A healthy drizzle of Dusseldorf mustard

INSTRUCTIONS

1. Toast two large pieces of sourdough.

2. Add a nice thick layer of the pulled beef brisket, while it's still warm, to one slice of bread.

3. With a butter knife, spread the Gournay cheese on the other slice of bread in an even layer.

4. Distribute the green onion slices in a healthy layer onto the cheese. Pat them down a little so that they stick to the cheese, making the sandwich easier to close later.

5. Add a layer of the shredded carrot on top of the onions.

6. Sprinkle the dried dill weed over the carrots.

7. Add a healthy drizzle of Dusseldorf mustard on top of the brisket.

8. Carefully close the sandwich by flipping the veggie side on top of the brisket side.

9. Cut the sandwich in half diagonally and enjoy!

Tip

For a different pop of flavor, try using fresh dill.

Some sandwiches are just excellent—perfect straightforward match-ups of the right flavors with the right textures.

10/10

The Merle

Episode 205 | AIRDATE: October 16, 2023 | PREP TIME: 20 minutes | Makes one sandwich

Just like its namesake, Merle Highchurch, Cleric of Pan, from the popular D&D podcast *The Adventure Zone*, this sandwich is a little quirky (and barely keeping itself together). Though its construction leaves a bit to be desired, it's hard to argue with the taste.

On top of an abundance of cheese (in the form of a slightly unhinged amount of Edam snack wheels), this sandwich features Canadian bacon. This meat has been a somewhat controversial addition to the Roll For Sandwich menu throughout the series, mostly due to its name. "Canadian bacon" is the American name for this particular type of cured pork loin. If you ask a Canadian about bacon, they are much more likely to think of peameal bacon. The term Canadian bacon comes from the days when Toronto was the pig-processing center of Canada, and New York City was importing cured pork loin and other pork products from Toronto. New Yorkers started calling this product Canadian bacon, and the name stuck—and spread throughout the rest of the country. Whatever you call it, we can agree that it's tasty!

While the individual components of The Merle are delicious on their own, the pan frying elevated this sandwich from pretty good to great, proving just how transformative heat can be for the sandwich experience. The McElroy Brothers from *The Adventure Zone* podcast were responsible for RFS season 5's Wild Magic table, and "Pan Fry in Butter" was arguably their best suggestion (if also one of the safest and least shocking). It seemed only fitting for this banger of a sandwich to be named after a character from the world they created.

INGREDIENTS

- 2 slices sesame sprouted grain bread
- 2 ounces Canadian bacon
- 4 mini Edam cheese wheels
- ¼ cup Old Bay pickle slices
- 1 ounce Dietz & Watson Steakhouse Pepper Mayo, or a suitable alternative

Tip

If you can't find or make Old Bay pickles, use regular dill pickles and sprinkle Old Bay seasoning on top after you've placed them.

INSTRUCTIONS

1. Place two slices of sprouted grain bread on a plate.

2. Place the slices of Canadian bacon on one slice of bread in an even layer. Canadian bacon is precooked, so there's no need to heat it up first (we'll do that later).

3. Unwrap the mini Edam cheese wheels and place them on top of the Canadian bacon in an even layer (as much as possible—I know we're getting a little wild here).

4. Arrange the sliced pickles in an even layer on top of the cheeses.

5. Squeeze the mayo onto the top slice of bread and spread it evenly with a knife.

6. Place the top slice of bread onto the rest of the sandwich, mayo side down.

7. Melt some butter in a frying pan over medium-high heat, and then add the sandwich on top of the butter. Add a small amount of water to the pan and cover it.

8. After a few minutes, flip the sandwich over. (This will be difficult with the Edam cheese wheels inside, as they may try to escape. I recommend pressing the sandwich between two spatulas to flip it.)

9. Re-cover and let the sandwich cook for a few more minutes. The goal is to melt the Edam without burning the bread.

10. Transfer the sandwich from the pan to a cutting board, cut it in half diagonally, and enjoy!

Pan frying this sandwich really helped it reach new heights of flavor.

10/10

The Demi Delhi-catessen

Episode 290 | AIRDATE: June 12, 2024 | PREP TIME: 5 minutes | Makes one sandwich

Sandwiches like this are the sandwiches I live for! There are days when the stars align, the dice are merciful, and I get to eat something that makes total sense for lunch. With the Demi Delhi-catessen, the dice were craving Indian, and boy did they deliver!

This sandwich is packed with so much flavor and spice. From the tandoori-spiced Gouda and achar masala pickles to the pizza seasoning and garlic chili crisp, it's a nonstop flavor parade. It was almost too much—with a different main, this could very easily have been overpowering. Luckily, chicken salad was perfect.

Chicken salad is kind of bland, all things considered—it's a relatively lean meat served cold and drenched in mayo—but in this sandwich, it is perfect. An unassuming star, it surrenders the spotlight while doing its best to support the more aggressive bits of the sandwich. It's the cleric in this sandwich party, with the mayo doing a great job of cooling off all the spice and moistening the crusty bread and drier chicken.

INGREDIENTS

- One 4"–6" (10.2–15.2cm) demi baguette
- ½ cup chicken salad
- 1 ounce tandoori Gouda
- ¼ cup achar masala pickle slices
- 2 large slices heirloom tomato
- Kosher salt
- Freshly ground black pepper
- Everything pizza seasoning, optional
- 1 tablespoon garlic chili crisp

Tip
If you can't find a demi baguette, use a section of a full baguette.

INSTRUCTIONS

1. Using a bread knife, slit the demi baguette down the side "hamburger style."

2. Spread the chicken salad in an even layer on the bottom half of the baguette.

3. Slice the tandoori Gouda and apply it in an even layer on top of the chicken salad.

4. Add the pickles in an even layer on top of the cheese.

5. Slice an heirloom tomato and place the slices on top of the pickles in an even layer.

6. Season the tomatoes with kosher salt and freshly ground black pepper. If you'd like to add the everything pizza seasoning, add it now. My original sandwich included it, but with so many other spices, it may not actually add much to the sandwich. Unless you are trying to re-create the sandwich as faithfully as possible, you can skip it.

7. Spread a few healthy spoonfuls of garlic chili crisp on the inside of the top piece of baguette.

8. Place the top piece of baguette on top of the rest of the sandwich sauce side down, cut it in half diagonally, and enjoy!

Tip
Finding achar masala pickles may be a challenge. If you can't, I suggest adding pre-made "pickle masala" powder to a jar of regular dill pickles.

Tip

Finding tandoori Gouda may be a challenge. If you can't, I suggest making ½ cup of your own tandoori masala spice mix and rubbing it on plain Gouda or sprinkling it over the chicken salad. Simply mix the following ground spices: 2 tablespoons coriander; 1½ tablespoons cumin; 1 teaspoon each garlic powder, ginger, cloves, mace, fenugreek, cinnamon, black pepper, and cardamom; and ½ teaspoon nutmeg.

Sometimes the dice dish up a combination that makes perfect sense—like a solid blend of Indian flavors.

10/10

The Crunch Squad

Episode 207 | **AIRDATE: October 20, 2023** | **PREP TIME: 5 minutes** | **Makes one sandwich**

This is by far the best-tasting sandwich to come out of my collaboration with The McElroy Brothers (of *The Adventure Zone* podcast). Each of the brothers contributed their fair share of horrific options to the roll list for season 5, but it wasn't all bad. They each added one thing that they considered to be a critical hit for a sandwich, and Sauce Up NYC's Almond Crunch Sauce was Justin's contribution.

This savory, garlicky sauce, packed with almonds, really is a killer addition to just about any sandwich. A rare "no roughage" roll also kept this sandwich fairly simple, and sometimes on this show, the less you roll, the better the odds of things working together. The somewhat spicy and sweet capicola and creamy Edam cheese laid down a perfect base for the almond crunch to then elevate. The Japanese mayo fit in perfectly, adding a bit more creaminess and richness.

The cinnamon bread (no raisins) added another subtle layer of complexity. The slight heat of the cinnamon fit perfectly with the capicola and almonds, giving an almost candied almond flavor without things being too sweet.

I owe Justin for turning me on to Almond Crunch Sauce and subsequently aiding in the creation of such a delicious sandwich . . . or rather, I would if he and his brothers weren't also responsible for putting me through some of the most heinous sandwiches of the show! I guess I'll call it even!

INGREDIENTS

- 2 slices cinnamon swirl bread
- 1½ ounces sweet capicola
- 1½ ounces Edam cheese
- ½ ounce Sauce Up NYC Almond Crunch Sauce, or a suitable alternative
- 1 ounce Japanese mayo

INSTRUCTIONS

1. Toast 2 slices of cinnamon swirl bread and lay them on a plate.

2. Place the sweet capicola slices on top of one piece of bread in an even layer.

3. Slice the Edam cheese into thin slices, then add them to the capicola in an even layer. Make sure to remove the wax coating from the Edam first if it has one.

4. Use a spoon to mix the almond crunch sauce from the bottom (it will have settled). Spread a few generous scoops of the sauce on top of the cheese.

5. Drizzle the other slice of bread with Japanese mayo, then spread it with a knife for even coverage.

6. Close the sandwich by placing the top piece of bread, mayo side down, on top of the rest of the sandwich.

7. Cut the sandwich in half diagonally and enjoy!

My collaboration with The McElroy Brothers was a wild ride, and The Crunch Squad was the highest moment!

This was the rare sandwich without any "roughage." Less was truly more in this case.

10/10

The Cheese Blessing

Episode 165 | **AIRDATE: June 21, 2023** | **PREP TIME: 20 minutes** | **Makes one sandwich**

Cheese may be the single greatest food that has ever existed. Any long-time fan of the show knows that I am a bit heavy-handed when it comes to cheese on my sandwiches. Sorry, not sorry. It's no wonder that a sandwich containing four different cheeses (and little else) scored a perfect 10!

There was a running joke in early 2023 about RFS having a "cheese curse." For an extended number of episodes, the dice just refused to give me cheese. After several sandwiches in a row spent in cheeseless desolation, I began to suspect that there were unseen forces at play. Surely it was more than random probability keeping me separated from my dairy delights! Luckily, the famine subsided, and we emerged together back into a promised land flowing with curds and whey.

This sandwich stands as a memorial to that terrible time in Roll for Sandwich history—a cheese blessing to counter the curse. May we never forget.

INGREDIENTS

- 2 slices sourdough bread
- 2 slices Muenster cheese
- ½ ounce espresso lavender aged cheddar
- ½ cup thinly sliced Granny Smith apple
- ½ ounce Butterkäse cheese
- Grated Parmesan cheese
- Italian herb blend
- A drizzle of Carolina-style barbecue sauce

INSTRUCTIONS

1. Place two slices of sourdough bread on a plate.
2. Place the Muenster cheese on one of the bread slices in an even layer.
3. Place slices of the espresso lavender cheddar on top of the Muenster.
4. Add the Granny Smith apple slices on top of the espresso lavender cheese.
5. Sprinkle the apples with the grated parmesan and the Italian herb blend.
6. Slice and place the Butterkäse on top of the seasoned apples.
7. Drizzle the other slice of bread with the Carolina-style barbecue sauce.
8. Close the sandwich by adding the top slice of bread sauce side down.
9. With the sandwich closed, add butter to the outside.
10. Preheat a pan over medium heat, then add the sandwich.
11. Add a small amount of water to the pan and cover it.
12. After a minute or two, flip the sandwich and recover it.
13. Once both sides are done and the cheese is melted, remove the sandwich from the pan and place it on a cutting board. Cut it in half diagonally and enjoy!

Four different cheeses? Enough said.

10/10

The Rotten Soldier

Episode 69 | AIRDATE: September 14, 2022 | PREP TIME: 5 minutes | Makes one sandwich

There are unlikely pairings in this series, and then there are sandwiches like this. Sandwiches I suspect no person in human history has created before this show. Japanese pickled plums and Norwegian whey cheese on the same sandwich? Only on Roll for Sandwich!

It's sandwiches like this that truly deserve to be included in this book, for posterity at the very least. The terrible and cursed combinations may make for entertaining videos, but the surprisingly good sandwiches—the ones that no one saw coming—are the ones that keep me coming back time and time again.

There are some strong flavors at play in this one, but thankfully, not every ingredient is punchy. Both the chicken and the cucumber are fairly mild, taking a back seat in the flavor profile. The first flavor powerhouse is the *umeboshi*, Japanese pickled ume fruit (often translated as "plum"), which has a very sour and salty, almost olive-like, flavor. It blends pretty well with the dill pickle mustard. The brunost, Norwegian caramelized whey cheese, brings in some much-needed sweetness (as does the honey wheat bread) to help offset all the sourness and saltiness.

The name of the sandwich comes from the show *What We Do in the Shadows*, where Matt Berry's character, Laszlo, calls someone his "sweet cheese." Despite having "rotten" in its name, this sandwich is a delightful surprise that I encourage you to try if you're feeling adventurous!

INGREDIENTS

- 2 slices honey wheat bread
- 1 ounce crunchy peanut butter
- 2 slices deli rotisserie chicken
- 1 ounce brunost cheese
- 3 umeboshi (Japanese pickled plums)
- ¼ cup sliced cucumber
- Everything bagel seasoning
- 1 ounce dill pickle mustard

INSTRUCTIONS

1. Toast two slices of honey wheat bread and lay them on a plate. (Bonus authenticity points if the bread is homemade or bakery-fresh! Mine was straight from another TikToker, @hannahbreadtok.)

2. Spread crunchy peanut butter on the bottom slice of bread.

3. On top of the peanut butter, layer the slices of deli chicken.

4. Add two thin slices of brunost on top of the chicken.

5. Remove the pits from the umeboshi and chop them into a paste. Spread the paste on the top slice of bread.

6. Add the cucumber on top of the brunost.

7. Sprinkle the everything bagel seasoning over the umeboshi paste.

8. Drizzle the dill pickle mustard on top of the cucumber.

9. Close the sandwich, flipping the top slice over so the umeboshi meets the mustard.

10. Cut the sandwich in half diagonally and enjoy!

Blending unique ingredients that might never come together otherwise (in this case, brunost and umeboshi) is part of the beauty of Roll for Sandwich!

The Rotten Soldier 29

10/10

Pure Dead Brilliant

Episode 332 | **AIRDATE: October 23, 2024** | **PREP TIME: 25 minutes** | **Makes one sandwich**

Roll for Sandwich has opened my eyes to so many foods from all over the world. This sandwich resulted from a special episode featuring many Scottish ingredients supplied by Ackroyd's Scottish Bakery here in Michigan. It was the first time I had heard of "butteries" and the first time I tried black pudding. These unknowns coming together to produce a 10/10 was a pleasant surprise for me and eye-opening for many viewers.

Aberdeen butteries are rich and flaky and set the stage for a great sandwich right from the start. The fried black pudding is earthy, salty, and full of wonderful spices like coriander and mace, which pair well with sweetness. The dice provided that sweetness in the form of the honey goat cheese, which also brings in a creaminess and tang. Layers of crunchy cucumber, though perhaps unexpected, give the sandwich a cool and refreshing element, helping to lighten everything up—and the crunch they add makes the sandwich a more interesting textural experience. Finishing with the honey mustard creates the perfect mix of sweetness, acidity, and spice to perfectly round out the flavors.

I was absolutely blown away by this combination. Compared to some sandwiches on this show, it was fairly simple, but the flavors together were anything but. If you have the opportunity to get your hands on everything you need to re-create this Scottish-inspired "piece," I suggest you do! I promise it will be "pure dead brilliant!"

INGREDIENTS

- 1 Aberdeen buttery
- 2–3 ounces black pudding, cut into ⅜" (1cm) slices
- Butter
- 2 ounces honey goat cheese
- ½ cup cucumber, thinly sliced
- Coarse kosher salt
- A drizzle of honey mustard

INSTRUCTIONS

1. Warm the Aberdeen buttery in the toaster or oven. Once warm, carefully slice the buttery in half bun-style. Lay the two halves cut sides up on a plate.

2. Fry the black pudding in a small amount of butter for a few minutes. Once fried, place an even layer of the black pudding slices onto the bottom buttery.

3. Crumble the goat cheese and add it to the top buttery.

4. Place even layers of cucumber slices on top of the black pudding. *Since this sandwich called for "extra cucumber," you'll need a few layers.*

5. Sprinkle the top cucumber layer with coarse kosher salt.

6. Drizzle honey mustard on top of the goat cheese.

7. Carefully flip the top half of the sandwich over onto the bottom half so that the honey mustard meets the cucumber. *Note: You will need to do this quickly to avoid losing any goat cheese.*

8. Cut the sandwich in half diagonally and enjoy!

Tip

Use room-temperature goat cheese, as it will be easier to break up without crushing your buttery.

This is a sweet and spicy homage to all things Scottish (with a few extra bits and pieces here and there). If your buttery is thinner than the one I used, try using two butteries instead—one as the top and one as the bottom.

10/10

The Peppadew® Pig

Episode 321 | AIRDATE: September 25, 2024 | PREP TIME: 10 minutes | Makes one sandwich

What an absolute banger of a sandwich! The dice really outdid themselves with this one. I'm a big fan of ribs but don't often order them when I'm out to eat because of how messy they are. Having them in sandwich form is just perfect. A rib sandwich is nothing new—there's of course the wildly popular, sporadically available, fast-food rib sandwich—but this is so much better than that.

While the fast-food sandwich comes topped with pickles and onions, the dice instead served up The Peppadew Pig with some pickled peppers and tomato, plus pepper-infused cheese. The peppers provide some acid to balance the fatty pork, but they also add a touch of sweetness that wouldn't otherwise be present since this "Pig" uses chipotle mustard instead of the gobs of barbecue sauce used on that *other* sandwich.

What you end up with is a rich, salty, savory sandwich somewhere between a rack of ribs and a cheesesteak. Heaven on sourdough!

INGREDIENTS

- 2 slices sourdough bread
- ½ pound precooked pork ribs in sauce
- 1 ounce Peppadew cheddar
- 3 slices fresh tomato
- 4–5 Peppadew peppers, sliced
- Scotch barrel smoked finishing salt
- 1 ounce chipotle mustard

Tip

If you have a hard time finding cheddar infused with Peppadew peppers, you can use regular cheddar and add extra peppers later.

INSTRUCTIONS

1. Toast two slices of sourdough bread and set them on a plate.

2. Remove the rib meat from the bones and reheat it. I usually just pop it in the microwave for a minute or two.

3. Once the meat is warmed, use a fork to spread it evenly on one of the pieces of toast.

4. Slice the cheddar and lay it on top of the rib meat in an even layer.

5. Use a kitchen torch to melt the cheese. I like to make sure the cheese gets a little charred on the edges whenever I use the torch.

6. Place the tomato slices on top of the cheese in an even layer.

7. Place the sliced Peppadew peppers on top of the tomato in an even layer.

8. Sprinkle the finishing salt on top of the peppers and tomatoes.

9. Spread a layer of chipotle mustard on the other slice of bread.

10. Close the sandwich by placing the top piece of bread sauce side down onto the rest of the sandwich.

11. Cut the sandwich in half diagonally and enjoy!

The melty cheese makes this sandwich. If you don't have a kitchen torch, build the sandwich without melting the cheese, and then pop the whole thing in the oven for a bit!

10/10

The Slawful Good

Episode 27 | AIRDATE: May 18, 2022 | PREP TIME: 10 minutes | Makes one sandwich

The Slawful Good, episode 27, was recorded after only a month of making Roll for Sandwich. At the time, I was making the show five days a week and everything felt like a whirlwind. I had been doing some pretty successful livestreams on TikTok and had even dubbed one of the sandwiches we created a perfect ten, but my audience at large, my regular viewers, still had yet to experience their first "perfect sandwich."

This was the episode that changed all that: The first time the stars aligned to give us a great lunch with no extra funny business. Far from a traditional pairing, it felt fitting after the first bite for this to be Roll for Sandwich's first official 10. When you break it down, it makes a lot of sense.

There are three different proteins, a somewhat rare occurrence for the show, and they surprisingly don't clash. The bread is sourdough, which I typically rate high, *and* includes cheddar cheese (we all know cheese makes everything better). The sandwich got buttered, which typically elevates a sandwich in both flavor and resilience against sogginess. The veggies were a little outside the box but not unwelcome—coleslaw, in particular, is an underrated sandwich addition, as anyone who has been to Primanti Bros. in Pittsburgh will tell you. Finally, red pepper jelly sent this sandwich over the top—a unique but perfectly viable sauce to bring it all together. It was truly Roll for Sandwich's first critical hit, and it's one worth trying at home!

INGREDIENTS

- 2 slices cheddar sourdough
- Salted butter
- 3 slices sandwich-cut pepperoni
- 2 slices deli chicken
- 1 slice sharp cheddar cheese
- ¼ cup coleslaw
- ¼ cup alfalfa sprouts
- 3 slices cooked bacon
- Red pepper jelly

INSTRUCTIONS

1. Toast and butter two slices of cheddar sourdough and lay them side by side on a plate.

2. Place three slices of pepperoni in an even layer on one of the pieces of bread.

3. Place the deli chicken on top of the pepperoni in an even layer.

4. Tear or cut the slice of sharp cheddar in half and layer the halves on top of the chicken.

5. Spoon the coleslaw on top of the cheese to create an even spread.

6. Layer the sprouts evenly on top of the coleslaw.

7. Wrap the precooked bacon in a paper towel and microwave it on high for around 20 seconds. All microwaves differ so be sure not to let it burn.

8. Once the bacon is warmed, add it on top of the sprouts in an even layer.

9. Spread the red pepper jelly generously on the buttered side of the other slice of bread.

10. Close the sandwich by placing the jellied sourdough slice jelly side down on top of the rest of the sandwich.

11. Cut the sandwich in half diagonally and enjoy!

Tip
You can use fresh bacon if you want, it will just take longer. Cook it using your preferred method.

This sandwich includes some of my favorite commonly underrated sandwich ingredients, including red pepper jelly, alfalfa sprouts, and coleslaw.

The Slawful Good

The Cusp of Greatness

More often than not, a sandwich comes close to perfection but misses the mark for one reason or another. Luckily, the reason is often identifiable, meaning that the sandwich can be remade even better. These sandwiches scored close to perfection on their maiden voyages, and now I leave it to you to perfect them!

9.9/10

The Comfortably Numb

Episode 113 | **Airdate:** January 23, 2023 | **Prep Time:** 5 minutes | Makes one sandwich

As with many sandwiches on Roll for Sandwich, this is 80 percent a normal deli sandwich, with just a slight twist at the end. For this one in particular, that twist elevates the sandwich to *almost* perfection. The Sichuan peppercorn is an unexpected addition but not an unwelcome one; the Chinese prickly ash has citrus notes that pair well with the tomato, cucumber, and the vinegary Florida-style barbecue sauce.

The Sichuan peppercorn also adds a unique experience element to this sandwich (especially if, like me, you add extra). The numbing effect it has on your tongue is not one you'll experience with many foods, but for some reason, I like it. It's a unique experience to bite into a sandwich and have your tongue go numb—one that perfectly fits within the chaos that is Roll for Sandwich!

INGREDIENTS

- 2 slices American pumpernickel bread
- 3 ounces roast beef
- 2 slices Swiss cheese
- 2 slices tomato
- ¼ cup cucumber
- 1 generous sprinkle of Sichuan peppercorn
- A healthy drizzle of Florida-style barbecue sauce

INSTRUCTIONS

1. Toast the slices of bread.
2. Top the bottom slice of bread with a generous layer of roast beef slices.
3. On top of the roast beef, add two slices of Swiss cheese.
4. On top of the cheese, add two slices of tomato.
5. Add a layer of cucumber slices on top of the tomato.
6. Sprinkle a generous amount of Sichuan peppercorn on top of the cucumber.
7. Add a healthy drizzle of barbecue sauce on the top slice of bread, spreading it with a knife for even coverage.
8. Carefully flip the top piece of bread over onto the rest of the sandwich, being careful not to spill the barbecue sauce in the process.
9. Cut the sandwich in half diagonally and enjoy!

The Sichuan peppercorn creates a one-of-a-kind sandwich experience.

9.7/10

The Toast Balone-y

Episode 135 | AIRDATE: April 10, 2023 | PREP TIME: 5 minutes | Makes one sandwich

This sandwich marked the first time I had ever tried pickled bologna, which may only surprise you if you are from Michigan like me, where it is *kind of a thing*. It wasn't a conscious decision to avoid it, I just never got around to it. That's one of the things I really love about this show—constantly trying new foods—and pickled bologna is absolutely bomb! I'm a sucker for pickles and pickled things in general and, while it may sound weird at first, bologna works so well pickled. Salty and fatty meat is best paired with acidic foods like tomato, mild peppers, or mayo—you need something tangy to cut the fat and really make your sandwich sing. Pickled bologna cuts out the middleman by bringing its own tanginess.

One ingredient that my American audience might not be familiar with is chicken salt. Chicken salt is a seasoning that is very popular in Australia. From the name, you might think it's something like bullion powder, but chicken salt doesn't contain any chicken, nor does it taste like chicken. (I got this wrong in the episode, but I've learned my lesson!) No, chicken salt is a garlicky salt filled with umami flavor. It was originally intended as a seasoning for rotisserie chicken, but now it gets used mostly for potato dishes like fries (or "hot chips," as they say down under).

I named this sandwich after Post Malone, who I weirdly connect to D&D, since I got into his music and D&D around the same time. I don't know if he's ever played, but I do know he's a big fan of Magic: The Gathering, a tabletop strategy card game that's owned by the same company. I also very much connect him to TikTok because he dropped a new album during the pandemic lockdown (which was when I was just getting into TikTok, in the dark times before Roll for Sandwich).

INGREDIENTS

- 2 slices sourdough bread
- 1 ounce pickled bologna
- ½ ounce pepperoni
- 2 slices provolone cheese
- ½ cup sliced cucumber
- ¼ cup sliced sweet and spicy pickles
- chicken salt
- 1 ounce piccalilli

INSTRUCTIONS

1. Toast the sourdough bread slices and place them on a plate.

2. Slice the pickled bologna into thin slices. Remove any artificial casing the bologna may have.

3. Place the sliced bologna on top of one slice of sourdough bread in an even layer.

4. Follow that with an even layer of pepperoni.

5. On top of the pepperoni, place the provolone cheese in an even layer.

6. Place the cucumber in an even layer on top of the cheese.

7. Add the pickles on top of the cucumber in an even layer.

8. Sprinkle with the chicken salt.

9. Spread the piccalilli on the top slice of bread in an even layer.

10. Close the sandwich by adding the top slice of bread, sauce side down, on top of the rest of the sandwich.

11. Cut the sandwich in half diagonally and enjoy!

Tip

You also might not be familiar with piccalilli. It's a classic UK relish of chopped, pickled vegetables in a mustard-based sauce. You can find it through online retailers, but also check the international section in your grocery store.

It's a bit amazing that this was my first time trying pickled bologna, but again, that's the beauty of Roll for Sandwich!

9.5/10

Sandwich a la King

Episode 314 | AIRDATE: September 9, 2024 | PREP TIME: 5 minutes | Makes one sandwich

Roll for Sandwich has given me really amazing and fun opportunities. I've gotten to travel and make sandwiches in some unexpected places, and it's always exciting when someone reaches out to invite me to come test my luck in a new locale. When the Michigan Renaissance Festival reached out to me about making a sandwich on location (and with the king, no less!), "Huzzah!" was all I could say.

Filming on location rather than in my kitchen always comes with its own set of challenges. There isn't as much time to fix things when they go wrong, and sometimes you just have to roll with the punches. Thanks to a strange typo during some back-and-forth with the venue in preparation for the event, mac and cheese somehow became "Mardari." When I got the list of ingredients, I was unfamiliar with this "mardari" and did my best in the short time I had before filming to do some internet research—of course, I came up with nothing. That should have been a red flag but, alas, the typo remained, and we ended up rolling it in the episode.

Luckily, it wasn't the end of the world. I learned something for next time, and the "mardari" was delicious!

INGREDIENTS

- 1 large chapati, or a suitable flatbread alternative
- 1 Scotch egg
- 2 slices Swiss cheese
- 1 slice tomato
- 2 ounces mac and cheese
- ½ ounce boom boom sauce
- King's sweat, optional

INSTRUCTIONS

1. Dress in your finest fantasy attire and travel to the nearest Renaissance festival.

2. Befriend the king.

3. Scour the land (festival) for ingredients.

4. After you've collected the ingredients, place the large chapati (or similar flatbread) on a plate.

5. Cut the Scotch egg in half and place it in the middle of the flatbread.

6. Add the Swiss cheese on top of the egg.

7. Add the tomato slice on top of the cheese.

8. Generously apply a scoop or two of mac and cheese on top of the tomato.

9. Drizzle on the boom boom sauce.

10. Fold the flatbread over to create a sandwich. Secure it with toothpicks and cut it in half.

11. Present your creation to the king. If he deems it worthy, he may crown it, bestowing it with some extra sodium from the sweat of his kingly brow.

Tip

You can make your own boom boom sauce by mixing ¾ cup mayonnaise; 2 tablespoons each ketchup, sweet chili sauce, and sriracha sauce; ½ teaspoon garlic powder; and ¼ teaspoon each onion powder, salt, and fresh ground black pepper.

Tip

This sandwich would benefit from more tomato slices, but my quest sadly afforded me only one.

If you want to be smart, cut the Scotch egg up even more so that you can distribute it more evenly and make it easier to close the flatbread. That's not what I did though …

The king crowning my sandwich—a true honor.

Sandwich a la King

9/10

Curd to the Wise

Episode 302 | **AIRDATE:** July 19, 2024 | **PREP TIME:** 10 minutes | **Makes one sandwich**

There are a lot of flowers you can eat. Many of the ornamental varieties we plant for their looks also happen to be edible. They often don't taste like much, but they can add a stunning visual to a salad or cocktail. We grew pansies a few years ago. They were meant to be decorative, but that didn't stop me from adding them to a sandwich! Pansies have a grassy taste and are not a substantial ingredient in any dish, but they do look nice, and they made this sandwich memorable.

Hands down, the key lime curd was the star of this one. Tart and rich, it played off the savory mix of meat and cheese nicely. Rolling a waffle for bread was kismet—the pockets made the perfect vehicle for the curd, and the sweet flavor balanced the curd's tartness. Lemon curd will probably be easier to find and should work well enough in re-creating this recipe, but the extra tartness of the key limes is worth the hunt if you have it in you to strive for perfect accuracy. I could see this sandwich on a fancy brunch menu at a trendy, seaside spot in the early summer. Give it a try and tell me you don't think the same!

INGREDIENTS

- 1 frozen waffle
- 1 slice sourdough bread
- 4 slices barbecue deli chicken
- 2 slices Muenster cheese
- ½ ounce pansy flower petals
- 1 kiwi
- Ground sage
- Key lime curd

INSTRUCTIONS

1. Toast one frozen waffle and one slice of sourdough bread, then lay them side by side on a plate.

2. Add the barbecue deli chicken slices on top of the sourdough in an even layer.

3. Place the slices of Muenster cheese on top of the chicken in an even layer.

4. Harvest the flowers from a few pansies. Wash them, pick off the petals, and spread them out on top of the cheese.

5. Peel and slice the kiwi and arrange it in an even layer on top of the cheese and pansies.

6. Sprinkle ground sage over the kiwi.

7. Spread the key lime curd on top of the waffle, filling the crannies.

8. Close the sandwich by placing the waffle, sauce side down, on top of the rest of the sandwich. (Depending on the sourdough you use, the waffle may not cover the entire sandwich. That's okay! Do your best!)

9. Cut the sandwich in half and enjoy!

The key lime curd and the waffle texture worked perfectly together.

9.5/10

Dim Sum Pair-O-Dice

Episode 269 | AIRDATE: April 15, 2024 | PREP TIME: 15 minutes | Makes one sandwich

I put wacky things on the list pretty often on Roll for Sandwich, but there are still plenty of things I don't think of. That's why I love the leftovers roll. It makes me think on my feet. At any given time in our house, I have one or two items in the fridge left over from other meals, mainly because I have two small children. (Anyone with small children knows that they have only two settings when it comes to food; either they want to eat *everything*, or they take one bite and are done with dinner.)

When the leftovers roll hits, I essentially have to go completely "off book." Anything I've added to the list has some thought behind it, but a leftovers roll means I have to open up the fridge and grab whatever is available, whether feasible for a sandwich or not. We've had dumplings, pasta, an entire taco . . . even soup! Clearly some have worked better than others.

Dumplings worked fantastically, and ended up paired with an interesting yet tasty mix of ingredients. The dumplings themselves were savory and salty, filled with pork, vegetables, and a nice broth (though having the broth does open up the chance of taking some "fire damage" when biting into the sandwich if you're not careful.) The super-sweet date and the sour cherry spread created a nice sweet-and-sour-sauce interplay that complemented the dumplings. The one possible drawback to this sandwich is that the cheese curds aren't really necessary, and their addition makes the sandwich a little unwieldy. Even so, the Dim Sum Pair-O-Dice (named for the viral TikTok song "Dim Sum Paradise" by OCT [On Company Time]) lives up to its name!

INGREDIENTS

- 2 slices sourdough bread
- 4 microwavable steamed pork dumplings
- 2 ounces fresh cheese curds
- 1–2 leaves romaine lettuce
- 1 date
- Steak seasoning
- 1 ounce sour cherry spread

INSTRUCTIONS

1. Toast the sourdough bread and lay the slices on a plate.

2. Prepare the dumplings according to the instructions printed on their packaging. (For added realism, offer them to your toddler for lunch. After your toddler inevitably takes a single bite, store them in the fridge for 24 hours before reheating.)

3. Spread the dumplings out on the bottom slice of bread.

4. Add the cheese curds in, around, and on top of the dumplings (wherever they will fit).

5. On top of the cheese curds, add an even layer of romaine lettuce.

6. Remove the pit from the date using a knife, then chop the date into a fine paste. Spread the paste on the other slice of bread.

7. Sprinkle a little steak seasoning over both halves of the sandwich.

8. Spread the sour cherry spread on top of the date spread.

9. Close the sandwich by flipping the slice with the spreads over on top of the lettuce, making sure the spread side is down.

10. Cut the sandwich in half diagonally and enjoy! (Watch out for hot juice inside the dumplings!)

Roll for Sandwich is the perfect means for using up leftover ingredients that might otherwise have gone to waste—in this case, some steamed pork dumplings.

Dim Sum Pair-O-Dice

9.9/10

The Swiss Near Miss

Episode 272 | AIRDATE: April 22, 2024 | PREP TIME: 25 minutes | Makes one sandwich

There is a relatively new tradition where I live here in Grand Rapids—a pop-up Christmas market is held downtown for a few weeks every December. A similar Christmas market, and likely the inspiration for our city's, has been held every year in Chicago since 1996. Both markets have a raclette stand, and my wife and I have created our own tradition of standing in line in the cold to get a raclette sandwich for dinner one December night each year. It is absolutely worth it. The cheese is cooked over a special grill and scraped directly from the wheel onto a crusty baguette. It's served with mustard, gherkins, and sometimes cured meats. It is heaven—stinky heaven—on bread.

Raclette is an odorous Swiss cheese. In Switzerland, it is usually served over boiled potatoes or on bread as street food (like at the market). I was able to find raclette once at a local shop, so I bought some to put it on the show. It is remarkable just how close my randomly generated sandwich came to the traditional ways of eating raclette. The potatoes, pickles, ham, and bread were all right at home with the stinky cheese. The only thing I lacked was the specialized grill. Even so, it turned out alright.

Though it doesn't quite rival the Christmas-time sandwiches fresh from the stall, the Swiss Near Miss is still a great at-home way to experience raclette. In the video, I put the cheese on too early. I've provided the instructions in a different order (adding the cheese at the end) to elevate this one to a full 10/10. If you can get your hands on some raclette, make this one—I promise the smell is worth it!

INGREDIENTS

- 2 slices sourdough bread
- 3 slices deli ham
- 1½ ounces raclette
- ½ cup leftover baked potato
- ¼ cup sour garlic pickles
- Finishing salt
- Salsa picante

INSTRUCTIONS

1. Toast the sourdough bread slices and place them on a plate.

2. Place the deli ham onto one slice of sourdough.

3. Reheat the leftover baked potato and spread the insides over the ham (do not include the skin).

4. Thinly slice the pickle and evenly layer the slices on top of the potato.

5. Sprinkle a pinch or two of finishing salt over the pickles.

6. Add several dashes of salsa picante on top of the seasoned pickles.

7. Preheat a pan on medium-high heat.

8. Thinly slice the raclette and add it to the hot pan. Melt the raclette, using a spatula to keep it moving.

9. Once the cheese is fully melted, remove the pan from the heat and pour the melted raclette directly from the pan onto the still-open sandwich.

10. Close the sandwich by adding the final slice of bread on top of the melted cheese.

11. Cut it in half diagonally and enjoy immediately!

Please recreate this sandwich with the new, improved instructions—and let me know how amazing it is as a 10/10!

9.6/10

The Elephant in the Room

Episode 162 | AIRDATE: June 14, 2023 | PREP TIME: 15 minutes | Makes one sandwich

Elephant ears are large flat pieces of dough that are deep-fried and usually covered with cinnamon and sugar or powdered sugar. The name varies from locale to locale, with some calling them beavertails, others fry bread or fried dough, but no matter what you call this fairground treat, it is always delicious!

One summer when I was at the fair with my family, I picked up a few extra elephant ears specifically to use on Roll for Sandwich. The dice landed on elephant ear for one of the grilled cheese special episodes and gave us this sandwich. It is probably the closest to a dessert sandwich that we have had on the show so far, with a couple of lucky rolls steering this in a very sweet direction. The Nat 20 sauce roll helped, allowing me to finish it off right with chocolate hazelnut spread.

The only element that doesn't really fit, and what kept it from scoring a 10/10 at the time was the savory Parmesan and Italian herb seasoning that just so happened to be sponsoring the video—awkward! The sandwich was ok with it, but honestly, it's better without it. The next time you're at the fair, snag an elephant ear and make this one . . . if you can resist eating the elephant ear long enough to get back home!

INGREDIENTS

- 1 elephant ear
- 2 slices provolone
- 2 slices Muenster
- Parmesan cheese, grated, optional
- Italian herb blend, optional
- ¼ cup mini marshmallows
- ¼ cup dried figs
- ½ ounce chocolate hazelnut spread
- Salted butter

INSTRUCTIONS

1. Cut the elephant ear in half. Aim to create two toast-size pieces. Place the two pieces onto a plate.

2. On one half of the elephant ear, layer the slices of provolone and the slices of Muenster cheese.

3. Optional: On top of the cheese, sprinkle grated Parmesan and the Italian herb blend. I would only do this if you are trying to replicate the sandwich exactly; otherwise, leave it off—the sandwich will be better for it.

4. Spread the mini marshmallows on top of the cheese in an even layer.

5. Chop the dried figs and evenly layer them on top of the marshmallows.

6. On the other piece of elephant ear, spread an even layer of the chocolate hazelnut spread.

7. Close the sandwich by putting the piece with the chocolate hazelnut spread on top of the rest of the sandwich with the spread side down.

8. Warm up the waffle maker and butter the inside.

9. Add the sandwich and carefully close the waffle maker as much as you can (it will probably not close all the way).

10. After a few minutes, once the cheese and marshmallows have melted, remove the sandwich from the waffle maker. The sandwich will be hot, so use silicone-tipped tongs to avoid burning yourself or scratching the waffle maker.

11. Enjoy!

This cheesy sweet mess was absolutely delicious—the dice were rolling lucky!

9.1/10

Taste of the Wild

Episode 159 | AIRDATE: June 7, 2023 | PREP TIME: 10 minutes | Makes one sandwich

My first introduction to the fiddlehead was the video game *Stardew Valley*. In the game, they are a seasonal forageable item that shows up in the Secret Woods and can be made into a risotto. Real fiddleheads grow all over the world, and, though they're a bit of a specialty item due to their seasonality, they are by no means a secret! Chefs all over the world have long been using fiddleheads as a gourmet ornamental vegetable because of their beautiful spiral shape, which is reminiscent of the head of a violin or fiddle.

Fiddleheads are the young, still-curled fronds of several species of fern. They have a relatively short harvest window in the spring when the plants are still new and the fronds haven't unfurled. Their scarcity in many regions makes them an expensive, gourmet item. Many of the fern varieties contain toxins that need to be cooked out before consumption. The taste is similar to asparagus.

Since I don't live in an area where fiddleheads are readily available in-season, I had not had a chance to try them before their appearance on Roll for Sandwich. A friend from New Brunswick sent me some both fresh and pickled, so I got to try them myself for the first time *and* introduce them to many in my audience at the same time. If you ever have the chance to try them, please do, and if you re-create this sandwich, you will be a part of an even rarer subset of people who have tasted them with Big Mac sauce and Tajín!

INGREDIENTS

- 2 slices white bread
- 4 slices salami
- 2 slices Swiss cheese
- ½ medium avocado
- 2 ounces pickled fiddleheads
- Tajín
- Big Mac sauce

Tip

If you want to make your own copycat Big Mac sauce, mix 1 cup mayonnaise; 1 tablespoon pickle relish; 2 teaspoons each white vinegar and mustard; and ½ teaspoon each smoked paprika, salt, and pepper.

INSTRUCTIONS

1. Toast the slices of white bread and place them side by side on a plate.
2. Place the salami on one slice of bread in an even layer.
3. Place the Swiss cheese on top of the salami in an even layer.
4. Remove the skin from the avocado half and mash the flesh up. Spread it on the other slice of toast.
5. Arrange the pickled fiddleheads in an even layer on top of the cheese.
6. Sprinkle the Tajín over both halves of the sandwich.
7. Drizzle the Big Mac sauce on top of the fiddleheads.
8. Close the sandwich by placing the avocado-spread piece of toast avocado side down on top of the rest of the sandwich.
9. Cut it in half diagonally and enjoy!

Mixing rare fiddleheads and Bic Mac sauce? Who'd have thought?

Fiddleheads have limited seasonality, so they're more of a gourmet item. They taste a bit like asparagus.

Festival of Seasons

There are times throughout the year when we take some time to relax and celebrate with those near and dear to us, times when we lay down our swords and take up flagons and feasting plates. Many traditional holiday foods and treats make their way onto Roll for Sandwich and are summarily disrespected as only the dice can do. This is an account of their stories. Happy feasting!

The Heart Attack

1.3/10

Episode 253 | AIRDATE: February 26, 2024 | PREP TIME: 10 minutes | Makes one sandwich

I can't tell you how many times one single ingredient completely tanks what was shaping up to be a great sandwich build. The Heart Attack should have been fairly serviceable. Sure, it would have been better with cheese and possibly a veggie with a little kick of spice or vinegar. True, soy sauce isn't as good of a choice here as, say, mayo or mustard, but it's not horrendous. But all that gets tossed out the window when the conversation hearts enter the chat.

Honestly, does anyone truly enjoy conversation hearts by themselves? I am fully convinced that they are only eaten out of the tradition and nostalgia associated with Valentine's Day. They are way too hard and don't even taste that great. Toss them in the middle of a sandwich, and you'll be lucky if you don't break a tooth. Rolling those hearts truly was the perfect parallel to a game of D&D. The party made it all the way through a dungeon full of monsters only to fail at checking the final chest for traps and being eaten by the mimic it truly was. Ah well, there's always the next sandwich!

INGREDIENTS

- 2 slices sourdough bread
- 2 ounces sliced pastrami
- ¼ cup sliced green pepper
- ¼ cup sliced Hungarian wax pepper
- ¼ cup conversation heart candies
- Soy sauce

INSTRUCTIONS

1. Place the slices of sourdough bread on a plate.
2. On top of one slice of bread, place the pastrami in an even layer.
3. Evenly layer the green pepper slices on top of the pastrami.
4. Evenly layer the slices of Hungarian wax pepper on top of the green pepper.
5. Add a layer of conversation heart candies on top of the wax pepper (or maybe don't—I can't really make you).
6. Drizzle soy sauce over the conversation hearts.
7. Close the sandwich by adding the other slice of bread.
8. Cut the sandwich in half diagonally and . . . enjoy?

What's the opposite of "Be Mine?" Whatever it is, that's this sandwich.

The Heart Attack

7.2/10

Sweet Summer Pie

Episode 295 | AIRDATE: June 24, 2024 | PREP TIME: 30 minutes | Makes one sandwich

Along with constantly trying to come up with new and interesting ingredients for the show, I'm also always looking for new processes and methods of preparing my sandwiches. Often, I dream up these methods and add them to the list without any sort of trial—that's part of the fun. If it turns out to be a disaster, at least it will be a fun video. I've toasted, grilled, waffle-ironed, even tried dollar-store sous vide (don't try this at home—it's a bad idea), so when summer rolled around, I thought I'd do what any good Midwestern dad would do: Toss it on the grill!

I couldn't foresee exactly what I'd end up having to toss on the grill and, well, the results were mixed. You see, a sandwich on normal bread would have been tenable. It would have been something akin to a literal grilled cheese rather than the pan-fried sandwiches that we usually call a grilled cheese. But, no, I had to roll oatmeal creme pies on *grilling* day. At room temperature, they are about one sneeze away from crumbling, so the addition of heat was not kind to them.

I at least had the foresight to wrap the sandwich in foil so the entire thing didn't just collapse and ruin my grill. What we ended up with was a slightly burnt, sort of caramelized pile of hot food that, in all honesty, didn't taste that bad. I've adjusted the instructions a bit to hopefully avoid the "slightly burnt" part, so if you doubt me, try the Sweet Summer Pie for yourself!

INGREDIENTS

- 2 Little Debbie Oatmeal Creme Pies, or a suitable alternative
- 1½ ounces corned beef brisket
- ½ ounce pepper jack cheese
- 1 ounce watermelon
- Barnacle Foods Bullwhip Kelp Hot Sauce, or a suitable alternative

INSTRUCTIONS

1. Unwrap the oatmeal creme pies and place them on a plate.

2. Layer the corned beef evenly on one of the oatmeal creme pies.

3. Slice the cheese and place it on top of the corned beef in an even layer.

4. Cut the watermelon into ¼" (6.5mm) thick slices and evenly layer them on top of the cheese.

5. Drizzle the hot sauce over the watermelon.

6. Place the other oatmeal creme pie on top and wrap the sandwich in aluminum foil.

7. Preheat your propane grill to 375°F (190°C), then place the aluminum foil–wrapped sandwich on the grill.

8. Close the grill and cook for 5 minutes.

9. Carefully remove the sandwich from the grill, open the foil, and eat with a knife and fork.

This one is a bit of a mess (heat does the oatmeal creme pies no favors), but it's a warm mix of interesting flavors that's definitely worth trying.

4.1/10

The Cold Day in Shell

Episode 211 | AIRDATE: October 30, 2023 | PREP TIME: 25 minutes | Makes one sandwich

It is incredibly evident that this sandwich was created the day before Halloween: It has both a little treat and a little trick. It is also the only sandwich (thus far) that I have had to put in the freezer, thanks to a suggestion from Griffin McElroy during the McElroy Family collaboration I did in 2023 (you'll remember them from *The Adventure Zone* podcast). The dice, who always have a sense of humor, even gave me a natural 20 on the sauce roll so I could try to salvage the sandwich. I think I did about as well as I could, choosing barbecue sauce to accompany the exterior chocolate sauce. Honestly, the sandwich would have fared much better during the rating portion had it not been frozen.

Alas, it *was* frozen, making it a truly difficult eating experience. There is a reason frozen sandwiches are not a thing (ice cream sandwiches notwithstanding). I still shudder when I think about it. This sandwich is one better left to the professionals (and by that I mean me, someone foolish enough to do this full-time).

INGREDIENTS

- 1 everything bagel, halved and toasted
- 3 slices sweet capicola
- 2 ounces queso fresco, crumbled
- 2 slices tomato
- ¼ cup sliced red onion
- 1 ounce barbecue sauce
- 1 ounce Smucker's Magic Shell® Chocolate Flavored Topping, or a suitable alternative

INSTRUCTIONS

1. Lay both bagel halves face up on a plate.

2. Place the capicola slices on the bottom half of the bagel in an even layer.

3. Crumble the queso fresco on top of the sweet capicola.

4. Layer a couple of slices of tomato on top of the cheese.

5. On top of the tomato, add a layer of red onion.

6. Spread an even layer of barbecue sauce on the cut side of the bagel top, then add the top to the rest of the sandwich, sauce side down.

7. Chill the sandwich by placing it in the freezer for 20 minutes.

8. Drizzle the Magic Shell on top of the sandwich. It should harden as it comes in contact with the cold sandwich. The top of the bagel should be glazed in the chocolate sauce.

9. Cut the sandwich in half and dig in . . . just be careful with your teeth!

Tomatoes really shouldn't even be refrigerated, but when you put them in the freezer, they become savory ice cubes... Not fun to eat!

The Cold Day in Shell

10/10

The PureBREAD

Episode 96 | AIRDATE: November 30, 2022 | PREP TIME: 5 minutes | Makes one sandwich

Ross Geller, from the sitcom *Friends*, is credited with inventing "The Moistmaker," a gravy-soaked piece of bread added to a Thanksgiving leftover sandwich to, well, make it moist. On this day in Roll for Sandwich history, the dice decided to give the Moistmaker a try, and, despite the surplus of carbs that resulted, the sandwich was a major success.

This sandwich is *a lot* of bread, it really is, but in this instance, that's okay. The yellow mustard as a finisher helps cut through all the heaviness of the bread and meat, adding a brightness that this sandwich desperately needed. Mustard alone may not have been enough, but thankfully the Moistmaker, the undeniable MVP of this sandwich, balances out what would otherwise have been a terribly dry sandwich. The extra slice of bread is an excellent vehicle for holding the extra gravy on the sandwich and not allowing it to just run off.

Thanksgiving leftovers are my favorite part of the holiday, and this sandwich elevates them to something you won't soon forget!

INGREDIENTS

- 3 slices rye bread
- 3 ounces warmed dark meat turkey
- 2 ounces warmed stuffing
- 2–3 ounces fresh mozzarella
- 3 ounces turkey gravy
- 1 ounce yellow mustard
- everything bagel seasoning, optional

INSTRUCTIONS

1. Toast two slices of the rye bread and lay them out on a plate. Set aside the third slice for later use.

2. Spread a healthy layer of dark meat turkey onto the bottom slice of bread. I find that shredding it works well for a sandwich.

3. Add a layer of stuffing on top of the turkey.

4. On top of the stuffing, add slices of the fresh mozzarella in an even layer.

5. Place the third slice of bread on a separate plate. Pour the turkey gravy over the bread, making sure to coat the entire slice. With a fork, flip the bread over and pour more gravy over the other side, making sure the bread is thoroughly soaked.

6. With tongs, add the gravy-soaked slice on top of the mozzarella. Feel free to scoop any leftover gravy that didn't soak into the slice onto the sandwich.

7. Drizzle yellow mustard on top of the gravy-soaked bread.

8. Optional: Sprinkle everything bagel seasoning on the sandwich.

9. Close the sandwich by adding the other toasted slice of bread on top.

10. Cut the sandwich in half diagonally and enjoy!

Bread on bread on bread might be just what this world needs more of.

0/10

How the Nog Stoll Christmas

Episode 233 | AIRDATE: December 22, 2023 | PREP TIME: 10 minutes | Makes one sandwich

If you were to leave this sandwich out on Christmas Eve instead of cookies and milk, you would most definitely be visited not by Santa Claus, but by the Grinch. Never has a sandwich so thoroughly denounced the ideals of "peace on earth, goodwill toward men" as this one. Each festive holiday element added to this sandwich only served to move it further from the true meaning of Christmas.

Stollen is a traditional German holiday bread, but it's much more like a cake. It's filled with nuts, dried fruits, and marzipan, and then coated with icing—it's not normally used to make sandwiches. This one was heavily saturated with rum, but unfortunately, that wasn't enough to numb me to this sandwich's horrors.

The sandwich insides themselves, divorced from their stollen prison, would have made a fairly good sandwich . . . almost. Bologna, cheese, lettuce, peppers—that's a nice balance of fat and acid. I can even forgive the barbecue sauce, which is a little sweet for that combination of ingredients in my opinion, but the sandwich took a nose dive at the Wild Magic roll (as is so often the case), when both marzipan *and* eggnog were rolled.

Adding the sweet, chocolate-covered almond confection took things in a wildly discordant direction, shoehorning in more "Christmas cheer," and then the sleigh's runners completely fell off when we had to dunk it all in eggnog before each bite. Oh, holy night! All I want for Christmas is a *different* sandwich.

INGREDIENTS

- Two ½" (1.3cm) thick slices rum stollen
- 2 slices bologna
- 1 slice Havarti
- ½ cup shredded lettuce
- 2 pepperoncini peppers
- 1 ounce dark chocolate–coated marzipan
- 1 cup eggnog
- Nutmeg
- Barbecue sauce

INSTRUCTIONS

1. Lay the stollen slices on a plate.

2. On top of one slice of stollen, place the bologna in an even layer.

3. Tear the slice of Havarti cheese in half. Lay the halves, one on top of the other, onto the bologna.

4. Spread the lettuce out on top of the cheese in an even layer.

5. Cut the top off of two pepperoncini peppers and squeeze the juice of the peppers onto the lettuce of the sandwich. Then, remove the stems and seeds from the peppers and slice the flesh into small rings.

6. Evenly layer the sliced pepperoncini on top of the lettuce.

7. Slice the marzipan into ½" (1.3cm) thick slices and arrange them evenly on top of the pepperoncini.

8. Drizzle barbecue sauce on top of the marzipan.

9. Close the sandwich by adding the other slice of stollen on top of the rest of the sandwich.

10. Pour the eggnog into a small dish or ramekin and sprinkle it with nutmeg.

11. Cut the sandwich in half diagonally. Eat it by dipping the end of the sandwich in the eggnog before each bite. Enjoy?

What's worse than a bad sandwich? A bad sandwich made soggy with eggnog!

The Nightmare Before Christmas

Episode 105 | **AIRDATE:** December 21, 2022 | **PREP TIME:** 5 minutes | **Makes one sandwich**

Is a sandwich a sandwich if it doesn't have any bread? Honestly, it's probably just a pile of ingredients on a plate. Even if I did still cut this one in half and eat it with my hands, it is, by just about every standard, only a sandwich in the very loosest of terms. So why include it in this book? Because this is a great example of the Roll for Sandwich formula working as intended. That may be surprising to hear, but it's true. Roll for Sandwich at its core is an *attempt* to make a sandwich, meaning that the potential for failure is baked into every aspect of the formula—even the "sandwich" part. In D&D, you make "skill check" rolls for things like stealth. If you fail your roll, you fail to be stealthy. In this case, we failed our roll *for sandwich*, so *failed* to even make an actual sandwich, adding to the humor of this episode.

This episode also happened to be the last episode before Christmas that year, and so I took it one step further and recorded the entire voiceover in the rhyme and meter of "'Twas the Night Before Christmas." It was a fun way to bring the year to a close, even if the "sandwich" left more than just bread to be desired that day!

INGREDIENTS

- 4 ounces barbecue jackfruit
- 1½ ounces cave-aged Gruyère
- ½ cup cucumber
- 1 peppermint candy cane
- 1 ounce ketchup

INSTRUCTIONS

1. Warm the barbecue jackfruit using your preferred method, then scoop several spoonfuls directly onto a plate.

2. Using an ostehøvel (a handheld Norwegian cheese slicer), slice the Gruyère thinly and add it in a layer on top of the jackfruit.

3. Slice a cucumber longways into thin slices and add it on top of the cheese.

4. With a mortar and pestle, crush the candy cane into dust. Sprinkle all the dust over the cucumbers.

5. Drizzle ketchup over the entire "sandwich."

6. Optional: Cut in half diagonally.

7. Optional: Eat with your hands.

8. Why are you still reading this? Please don't make this.

The dice seem to equate the holidays with a time of true horror. This mix is not one to replicate.

0.5/10

The H.O.A.

Episode 231 | AIRDATE: December 18, 2023 | PREP TIME: 10 minutes | Makes one sandwich

With how Christmas sandwiches have treated me on this show, you would think I was a permanent member of Santa's Naughty List. Something about the festive season has always seemed to produce sandwiches that go horribly, horribly wrong, and The H.O.A. was no exception.

To be fair, I am the one who added the gingerbread house kit to the list of possible bread options, but such is the nature of my quest. I must at once be Dungeon Master, scheming and plotting dubious creations, and Player, trying to navigate the dungeon of dastardly deli-fare unscathed.

Even though certain ingredients seem doomed from the start, it really is the combinations that make or break a sandwich. In this case, while the gingerbread was bad, the addition of tuna was worse, and the peppermint candy cane was the nail in our Christmas coffin. Hopefully, your morbid curiosity only extends to reading about this monstrosity, but if you decide to re-create it . . . don't say I didn't warn you!

INGREDIENTS

- 1 gingerbread house kit, including gingerbread, icing, and decorative candy
- One 5-ounce can albacore tuna
- 2 slices salami
- 2 slices Swiss cheese
- 1 plum
- 1 green onion
- 1 peppermint candy cane
- 2 tablespoons Colman's Mint Sauce, or a suitable alternative

INSTRUCTIONS

1. Begin by opening the gingerbread house kit and placing a toast-sized piece of gingerbread on a plate. You may need to cut the gingerbread down to size or do your best to combine multiple pieces of gingerbread depending on the kit you're using. Set aside the rest of the gingerbread and the other contents of the kit for later.

2. Open the can of tuna and drain the juices, then use a fork to add tuna to the top of the gingerbread until it forms an even layer.

3. Add the slices of salami on top of the tuna in an even layer.

4. Add the slices of Swiss cheese on top of the salami in an even layer.

5. On a cutting board, cut the plum into slices, being careful to remove the pit as you do. Add the slices of plum on top of the Swiss cheese until they form an even layer.

6. Chop the green onion into small rings, and then add a decent handful on top of the plums.

7. With mortar and pestle, crush the candy cane into a gritty dust and add it on top of the plums and onions.

8. Drizzle the mint sauce on top of the crushed candy cane.

9. Close the sandwich by adding another layer of gingerbread on top.

10. Using the icing and candies from the gingerbread house kit, decorate the top piece of gingerbread. You can pipe the icing straight from the bag by cutting the corner off the bag to create a small hole. Use the icing to stick the candies to the gingerbread.

11. Whether to cut this sandwich is entirely up to you. I would advise against it, but, well . . . I advised against making this sandwich in the first place—so, you know, go nuts.

12. *Bone apple teeth!*

This sandwich starts with a potentially horrible flavor pairing: sweet and fishy. With the layering on of savory and minty ingredients, it just gets worse and worse.

Epic Failures

I feel like I am pretty skilled at seeing the good in things. I am generally a glass-half-full kind of guy. I've applied this philosophy to my sandwich analyses, as well. Some may call me "too forgiving" of the wild and wacky combinations created on the show, but who can blame me? They are sort of my children, after all (RIP Tom). Sometimes, though, there are no redeeming qualities. Sometimes, the only solution is to cast the unholy ingestible into the fire and pray for forgiveness to the powers that be for what I have created. These are the "Nat 1s," the "Critical Failures," the "sandwiches that never should have been." Abandon all appetite, ye who enter here.

DISCLAIMER: The following sandwiches have been recorded herein for posterity and historical purposes only and are not intended, in any way, to be re-created and subsequently consumed with your own human mouth (or the mouths of your children, pets, friends, or even enemies). Roll for Sandwich takes no responsibility for any retching, stomach woes, or massive self-loathing that may occur as a result of doing so. **You have been warned.**

0/10

The Failed Stealth Check

Episode 64 | **AIRDATE:** August 31, 2022 | **PREP TIME:** 5 minutes | **Makes one sandwich**

Let me be 100 percent clear. *This is not a good sandwich!* I considered it the worst sandwich the show produced for several seasons afterward. It was the first sandwich that I debated fully tapping out on, but I stuck to my guns and finished the darn thing. I don't know if that makes me brave or stupid . . . it's probably both.

Sardines don't belong on a sandwich. On a cracker? Sure. But not on a sandwich. There were also way too many of them on this one, and the sardines packed in oil were particularly strong in the fishiness department, since they didn't have a flavored marinade to help take the edge off. I was hoping for some stronger flavors from the other rolls to help camouflage the taste, but, alas, the dice had other plans.

The failed camouflaging of the flavors is where the name of the sandwich came from, attempting to use the D&D stealth skill, and (like this sandwich) failing spectacularly. I still have nightmares about this sandwich, and, even after hundreds of other episodes, I still count it among the worst.

INGREDIENTS

- 2 slices Italian bread, toasted
- 7–8 canned sardines packed in extra-virgin olive oil
- 2 slices Muenster
- ¼ cup sliced cucumber
- 1–2 leaves iceberg lettuce
- 1 ounce pickled ginger strips
- 1 ounce avocado ranch

INSTRUCTIONS

1. Place the Italian bread slices on a plate.

2. Open the tin of sardines and drain off some of the oil. Use a fork to set the sardines on one slice of the bread, spreading them out as much as possible.

3. On top of the sardines, layer the Muenster cheese.

4. Add the cucumber slices on top of the cheese.

5. On top of the cucumber, layer the lettuce leaves. You can break them into pieces or leave them whole if you prefer.

6. Add the pickled ginger strips on top of the lettuce. You can use pink or white ginger, whichever you prefer—the taste will be the same.

7. To the top slice of bread, add the avocado ranch. I recommend spreading it with a knife to get an even layer.

8. Close the sandwich by adding the top slice of bread, ranch side down, to the sandwich.

9. Cut it in half diagonally and think about what you've done!

Tip

If you do decide to brave this sandwich, and have trouble finding pickled ginger, check your local Asian grocery store.

WARNING!

Smelling, looking at, or otherwise consuming this sandwich is done at your own risk. Roll for Sandwich does not recommend *any* sandwich with a score of 0/10 and retains no responsibility should you venture the risk.

This sandwich really has no redeeming qualities.

0/10

The Abomination

Episode 59 | **AIRDATE: August 19, 2022** | **PREP TIME: 10 minutes** | **Makes one sandwich**

No particular ingredient in this sandwich is all that heinous. The problem is the combination, and the portions don't help. Within the Roll for Sandwich process, there are a few opportunities for "extra" items to be rolled—extra main ingredients, extra veggies, etc.—and in this instance, they all hit at once. Not only was one extra main rolled, but a second extra main was also rolled *and* an extra veggie.

The result was the aptly named Abomination, which combined not one but two vegan chicken patties with leftover hot dogs (an ironic twist in and of itself) and several strong-tasting toppings. Garlic, olives, horseradish flavor from the wasabi . . . it was a lot. And to top it off (literally), everything was barely contained within an English muffin, one of my least favorite breads.

The dice were in quite a mood when they designed this one. In my excitement at receiving handmade dice with little sandwiches inside, and having rolled a good sandwich on their first use, I decided to "let it ride," using the same set of dice two times in a row, not something typically done on Roll for Sandwich. Perhaps I had already exhausted all the luck in the dice or had angered the dice gods with my hubris, but either way, this was the result. Something no one asked for, hot dogs and vegan meat. A true Abomination.

INGREDIENTS

- 1 English muffin
- 2 vegan chicken patties
- 1–2 hot dogs
- 2 slices Muenster
- 6 hamburger dill pickle slices
- 6 small pimento-stuffed green olives
- Pickled garlic
- Salt and pepper
- 1 ounce wasabi sauce

INSTRUCTIONS

1. Separate one untoasted English muffin into its two halves and place them face up on a plate.

2. Prepare the vegan chicken patties according to the package, and, once warmed, place them on one of the muffin halves. (Yes, *both* of the patties. I know—it's cursed.)

3. Prepare the hot dogs using your favorite method. Once warm, slice them longways and place them on top of the vegan chicken patties.

4. Pray to whatever deity you think will listen.

5. On top of the hot dogs, add the cheese in a single layer.

6. Add the pickle slices in a layer on top of the cheese.

7. Slice the olives in half longways (to give them a fighting chance of staying on the sandwich). Place the olive slices in a layer on top of the pickles.

8. Using a garlic rocker, smash two cloves of pickled garlic. Add the smashed garlic to the top English muffin half. The crannies of the muffin should provide ample opportunity for the garlic to find purchase and not fall off.

9. Add a light sprinkle of salt and pepper to the bottom half of the sandwich (because *that* will surely help).

10. Add the wasabi sauce to the top muffin half on top of the garlic and spread it with a knife. The sauce will also seep into the crannies of the muffin.

11. Add the freshly sauced top of the muffin, sauce side down, to the rest of the sandwich.

12. Cut the sandwich in half and deal with the consequences of your actions.

Vegan chicken patties with hot dogs? Wasabi and pickled garlic? This sandwich disaster is a lot.

The Abomination

The Crabomination

0/10

| Episode 323 | AIRDATE: September 30, 2024 | PREP TIME: 5 minutes | Makes one sandwich |

At the time of writing, the Crabomination reigns supreme as my least favorite sandwich* I've had to endure on the show. I can only hope that it's still the worst but, knowing my luck (and my propensity to torture myself with my ingredient lists), that's highly unlikely.

This sandwich is particularly heinous for a few reasons. The first is taste. I have a hard time with very fishy flavors. I enjoy seafood, but when the flavor is particularly strong, it activates something primal within me that gets my skin crawling. I don't know what it is—maybe memories of fishing with my dad as a child, holding on to a slimy fish, working the hook out of the mouth (shudder)—whatever the reason, the taste and smell of very fishy things is an immediate turnoff for me. And these little crabs might be the fishiest thing I've ever tasted.

The second, and possibly more damning thing about this sandwich, is the texture. The tamago gani (dried crab snacks) are small whole crabs (shell and everything), and even though they are dried, the shells are still very crunchy. They are crunchy in a way that almost seems inedible; like you are making a mistake putting them in your mouth. They are not hard enough to hurt your teeth when you bite them, but they break into small pieces that do not fully dissolve when you chew. It's almost like eating eggshells. Biting into a relatively soft sandwich, and then periodically finding bits of shell with your teeth is an experience I don't wish on anyone.

I know that some people enjoy tamago gani, and that's awesome! I never want to begrudge anyone foods they enjoy, especially when those foods come from a culture that is different from my own. I am aware that I exist with biases from the foods I was raised on, and what I consider to be "normal" is solely based on my specific worldview. This might be the perfect sandwich for you. I doubt it, but it might be! If you choose to find out, you do so at your own risk!

*There was a worse overall episode, but I won't spoil the surprise . . .

INGREDIENTS

- 2 slices Italian bread
- 4 ounces pickled bologna
- 2 ounces brunost, thinly sliced
- ¼ cup sliced pickles
- 1 ounce tamago gani (Japanese dried crab snacks)
- 1 ounce ketchup

INSTRUCTIONS

1. Place the slices of Italian bread on a plate.

2. Slice the pickled bologna off the ring in ⅜" (1cm) thick slices, making sure to remove any artificial casing. Lay the bologna slices on the bottom slice of bread in an even layer.

3. Add the brunost on top of the bologna. I recommend using an ostehøvel (a handheld Norwegian cheese slicer) to cut the brunost nice and thin.

4. On top of the brunost, add sliced pickles in an even layer.

5. Place the tamago gani in an even layer on top of the pickles.

6. Drizzle the ketchup over the crabs.

7. Cut the sandwich in half diagonally and brace yourself! Remember, no one forced you to make this . . .

Tamago gani might be your favorite snack—I'd still probably recommend against adding any to your sandwiches.

The Crabomination

All Taffy, No Laughy

0/10

Episode 301 | AIRDATE: July 17, 2024 | PREP TIME: 10 minutes | Makes one sandwich

When sandwiches like this premier on the show, I inevitably get asked, "What possessed you to put that as an option? How would that ever work on a sandwich?" My response to that question varies by the day, depending on how snarky I'm feeling. The following is the real answer.

I did *not* expect taffy to work in a sandwich. Ever. There are sometimes options on the lists that are almost guaranteed to fail, and that's by design. I approach the show in the role of two distinct characters. There is Jake the Player, who rolls dice and tests his fate against the dice gods in the hopes of creating a memorable and tasty sandwich from the chaos, and there is Jake the Game Master. The Game Master's job is to facilitate joint storytelling. In this case, Jake the GM throws challenges at Jake the Player so that he can claim victory or suffer defeat. For the GM, either result is good, because both tell a story—and a story without conflict isn't much of a story at all.

I think the drama of this dynamic is what keeps people coming back. Will his sandwich be delicious or incomparably cursed? In this case, it was the latter. Don't put taffy on your sandwiches unless you take some kind of sick pleasure in pulling out your own fillings. And if you do, then, I guess, go for it! Who am I to judge? You see what I put myself through.

INGREDIENTS

- 2 slices wheat bread, toasted
- One 7½ ounce can Simmenthal beef in gelatin, or a suitable alternative
- 1 ounce Liptauer cheese spread
- 1 small kiwi
- 1–3 lettuce leaves
- 3 pieces saltwater taffy
- 1 ounce pad thai sauce

INSTRUCTIONS

1. Lay the toasted wheat bread on a plate.

2. With a butter knife, spread half the can of beef in gelatin onto the bottom slice of bread. Set the rest of the can aside, it will not be used in this recipe.

3. Spread the Liptauer cheese spread on the other slice of bread.

4. Slice the kiwi into thin slices and place them on top of the beef in an even layer. Optional: Remove the kiwi skin with a potato peeler prior to slicing.

5. Place the lettuce on top of the kiwi. (The type of lettuce you use is up to you. I used a red lettuce fresh from my garden.)

6. Unwrap the saltwater taffy. (The flavor of the taffy isn't that important, since there is no good option here.)

7. To the best of your ability, slice, chop, or otherwise mangle the taffy into smaller pieces, and then place them on top of the lettuce. (Be careful, taffy does not cut well. For maximum safety, use a chainmail cut glove like mine!)

8. Drizzle pad thai sauce over the taffy, and then add the other slice of bread on top.

9. Carefully cut the sandwich in half diagonally. It probably won't work but do your best.

10. I guess you have to eat it now . . .

Saltwater taffy on a sandwich: A true "gift" from Roll for Sandwich GM Jake to Roll for Sandwich Player Jake.

The Nasty Patty

Episode 307 | **AIRDATE: August 19, 2024** | **PREP TIME: 35 minutes** | **Makes one sandwich**

It is fairly common for the dice to pair ingredients with clashing flavors, but it is rare for every single item on the sandwich to be at odds with each other. The Nasty Patty managed to accomplish this at every turn. It's the epitome of disjointed flavor combinations. Some of these items could have been redeemed by a different main ingredient, but on a fish sandwich—they just don't work.

The texture of this sandwich is somehow even worse than the taste—think "biting into fiberglass insulation." This wasn't the first time I tried to make cotton candy work on a sandwich. The previous attempts all ended somewhat anticlimactically, with the cotton candy completely dissolving and leaving behind just a coating of flavored sugar. This time, I opted to use a lot more cotton candy because I needed to see if that texture being part of the actual sandwich-bite experience could improve things. It did not, though it did make for an amusing cross section!

INGREDIENTS

- 2 slices cinnamon raisin bread, toasted
- 1 frozen, breaded Alaskan pollock patty
- 1½ ounces sweet piquant pepper cheddar, sliced
- ½ ounce fresh basil leaves
- ½ ounce spicy jalapeño cotton candy
- 1 ounce ketchup

INSTRUCTIONS

1. Place both slices of cinnamon raisin bread on a plate.

2. Prepare the frozen fish patty according to the instructions on the packaging. *Note: The brand I used took about 15 minutes in an oven set to 425°F (218°C), but yours may vary.*

3. Place the prepared fish patty on the bottom slice of bread.

4. Place the cheese slices on top of the warm fish patty. *Note: The thinner the cheese is sliced, the more likely it will be to melt a bit.*

5. Add a layer of fresh basil leaves on top of the cheese.

6. Use your hands to form the cotton candy into a patty, and place it on top of the layer of basil.

7. Squeeze ketchup onto the top slice of bread.

8. Close the sandwich by putting the top slice of bread on the cotton candy, ketchup side down.

9. Cut in half diagonally and serve immediately, before the ketchup dissolves the cotton candy (and before you have time to reconsider your life choices).

You may be thinking to yourself, "those eggs look delicious." Please know that those are thick patties of spicy jalapeño cotton candy. And they were not delicious on this sandwich.

The Nasty Patty

Beanhamut

0/10

Episode 140 | AIRDATE: April 21, 2023 | PREP TIME: 10 minutes | Makes one sandwich

The Beanhamut is a parade of strange ingredients, and for Roll for Sandwich, that's really saying something! It also happens to be vegetarian, but I don't really think that selling point is enough to redeem this particular creation. The "star" of the sandwich, if you can call it that, is a healthy portion of baked beans—and not just any ol' baked beans, mind you, but beans flavored with Dr Pepper®. Someone took a sip of their soda, and 23 flavors just wasn't enough. They truly thought, "You know what this needs? A disproportionate amount of bean flavor!" Well, RFS saw their 24-flavor combo and added even more.

The bread being cherry bread was actually fairly on theme for a soda-flavored sandwich. It was like a sweet brioche swirled with cherry and topped with frosting, definitely less of a sandwich bread than a breakfast or even dessert bread. More tart cherries are produced in Michigan than anywhere else in the United States. There's even a yearly cherry festival in Traverse City. If you spend any length of time in Michigan, you're bound to run into some cherry-inclusive specialty goods, so when I saw this bread in my local supermarket, I grabbed it for the show. My apologies if it's hard to find a suitable bread to re-create this sandwich—you should have no trouble finding blue Takis® at just about any gas station, though!

INGREDIENTS

- 2 slices cherry bread
- 2 ounces Serious Bean Co. Dr Pepper Baked Beans, or a suitable alternative
- 1 ounce Red Dragon Cheddar Cheese with Wholegrain Mustard & Ale, or a suitable alternative
- ¼ cup Kühne Whiskey Cornichons, or a suitable alternative
- ½ cup Takis® Blue Heat, or a suitable alternative
- Jalapeño ketchup

INSTRUCTIONS

1. Place the slices of cherry bread on a plate.

2. Warm the beans using your preferred method. Once warmed, spoon the beans onto one slice of bread in an even layer.

3. Slice the cheese and place it on top of the beans in an even layer.

4. Place the cornichons on top of the cheese in an even layer.

5. Place the Takis on top of the cornichons in an even layer.

6. Drizzle the jalapeño ketchup on the remaining piece of bread.

7. Close the sandwich by placing the top piece of bread, ketchup side down, onto the rest of the sandwich.

8. Cut it in half diagonally and . . . enjoy?

This is an unusual blend of ingredients you wouldn't think would work—sweetness, baked beans, pickles, spice. And you'd be right.

Beanhamut

0/10

Deck the Halls

Episode 348 | AIRDATE: December 9, 2024 | PREP TIME: 15 minutes | Makes one "sandwich"

I don't know what it is about Christmas that brings out the absolute worst in the dice. Perhaps it is the fact that I typically take at least a few weeks off after Christmas, and the dice know it's their last chance to terrorize me for a while. Maybe they are little agents of Krampus, bent on punishing me for the other sandwich sins I've committed throughout the year. Whatever the reason, as December 25 creeps closer and closer, the chances that I encounter an unholy monster of a sandwich exponentially rise.

You may not even be able to call Deck the Halls a sandwich, but it is still one of the worst things the dice have wrought. On Roll for Sandwich, we are always attempting to make a sandwich by rolling dice, but sometimes we fail at the "sandwich" part. On this day, we failed to sandwich and smoothied instead.

Meat should never be part of a smoothie. Neither should garlic. This had both and then some. Appropriately, the meat was reindeer, not just because it was December but because I had been gifted some during a trip to Iceland. I apologize to the lovely person who gave me that gift, but you have to know that anything you give me may or may not end up becoming part of the worst imaginable food experiences.

I hope and pray that this smoothie remains the peak of horror for the show because I'm having a hard time imagining what could possibly unseat it, and that is truly terrifying!

INGREDIENTS

- ¼ cup reindeer pâté
- ¼ cup water chestnuts
- 2 tablespoons toum (Lebanese garlic sauce)
- 1½ cups ice
- 1 cup water

INSTRUCTIONS

1. In a blender, combine the reindeer pâté, water chestnuts, toum, ice cubes, and water.

2. Blend until smooth. (Well, as smooth as you can make it.)

3. Pour into a glass and drink with a boba straw.

4. Please don't.

This barely qualifies as a "sandwich," but it definitely qualifies as something you should not make.

0/10

The Bad Buddy

Episode 41 | **AIRDATE:** June 9, 2022 | **PREP TIME:** 10 minutes | Makes one sandwich

There are peaks and valleys, and The Bad Buddy was the first time we hit rock bottom. In the first 40 episodes, I'd given out a score of 1/10, even went as low as 0.5/10, but in each of those sandwiches, I'd still found some glimmer of redemption.

The Bad Buddy, or just "Episode 41" as it was at the time, slapped me across the face in a way that left *no* room for hope. I made it 80 percent to a normal sandwich only to be hit with two polar opposite but equally strong flavor options right at the end. The cookie butter, though great on toast or perhaps with some fruit jam, was *not* a welcome addition to the salami, cheese, and vinegary vegetables. It's a shame, since I grew up on speculoos, or "Dutch windmill cookies," as I knew them as a child. What was worse, though, was the furikake, which is mostly seaweed and has a fishy taste. There are few more jarring flavor contrasts than sweetness and fish, which, unfortunately, I've experienced too many times to count on this show.

There was one silver lining to this sandwich. This stinker inspired another TikTok account from the UK, *@furrifingers*, to make a sandwich puppet modeled after it! With the help of the RFS community, I named him Buddy (which sounds like "butty"—British slang for sandwich or roll). It's still one of the coolest pieces of mail I've ever received!

INGREDIENTS

- 1 mini croissant
- 4 slices salami
- 2 slices smoked Gouda
- ¼ cup banana pepper rings
- ¼ sliced red onion, marinated in pickle brine
- Furikake
- Speculoos cookie butter

Proof that even a terrible sandwich can be inspiring: Buddy the puppet is much more appealing than The Bad Buddy sandwich.

INSTRUCTIONS

1. With a bread knife, cut the mini croissant in half hamburger bun–style and set the two halves side by side on a plate.

2. On the bottom half of the croissant, place folded slices of salami in an even layer.

3. Fold the slices of smoked Gouda in half and place them on top of the salami in an even layer.

4. Arrange the slices of banana pepper evenly on top of the cheese.

5. Evenly layer the marinated red onion slices on top of the banana peppers.

6. Sprinkle the onions and peppers with the furikake.

7. On the other half of the croissant, spread the speculoos cookie butter to cover the full surface.

8. Close the sandwich by placing the top half of the croissant cookie butter side down onto the rest of the sandwich.

9. Cut this monster in half and dig in.

Just another day of mixing the sweet and cheesy flavors I love with the fishiness I'd rather avoid.

The Bad Buddy

5/10

The Descent Into Avernus

Episode 242 | **AIRDATE: January 29, 2024** | **PREP TIME: 10 minutes** | **Makes one sandwich**

I don't have the biggest spice tolerance, mostly due to digestive issues. It's a bummer because I love the tastes of many different kinds of spicy foods. Still, in my day to day, I typically avoid it. That hasn't stopped me from featuring some items on the show that are spicier than I would normally eat. When I do, I just try and space them out, so I'll have time to recover. Unfortunately, the dice sometimes just love a big old dogpile.

This is one of the spiciest sandwiches that has been on the show. Even down to the Spanish chorizo, the spice was out in full force. You may have thought the main was pepperoni if you've never seen Spanish chorizo, and to be fair, it is a similar cured sausage, but it is not the same. You also might not recognize it if you are more familiar with Mexican chorizo. Rather than being cured and sliced thin, Mexican chorizo is sold ground and mixed with spices, so the form is quite different. Even if it had been pepperoni, it would have been an equally rocky start since I typically avoid that, as well.

Other than the cheese, which tried its best to bring some relief, with each ingredient we descended further and further into a spicy infernal hellscape (Avernus is the D&D-lore equivalent of hell). On any other day, an entire fresh habanero would have been enough to seal my fate, but to then add chili crisp and Caribbean jerk sauce? The dice couldn't help but kick me while I was down. I suffered my self-imposed fate, though, as I always do for this show, and the sandwich at least tasted very nice. However, a rating of 5 seemed fair knowing the pain that would soon follow.

INGREDIENTS

- 2 slices sourdough
- Sliced Spanish chorizo
- 2 slices Muenster
- 1 green onion, sliced
- 1 small fresh habanero pepper, seeds and ribs removed, thinly sliced
- 1½ tablespoons garlic chili crisp
- Caribbean jerk hot sauce

INSTRUCTIONS

1. Place the slices of sourdough bread side by side on a plate.

2. Arrange the slices of chorizo on one slice of bread in an even layer.

3. Place the slices of Muenster cheese on top of the chorizo in an even layer.

4. Arrange the green onion slices in an even layer on top of the cheese.

5. Layer the habanero slices evenly on top of the cheese and onions.

6. Generously drizzle with the garlic chili crisp.

7. Drizzle the top slice of bread with Caribbean jerk hot sauce.

8. Close the sandwich by adding the top piece of bread, sauce side down, on top of the rest of the sandwich.

9. Cut the sandwich in half diagonally and prepare to burn!

This was a spicy, spicy inferno of a sandwich. Good flavors, but a bad afternoon.

The Descent Into Avernus

0.8/10

I'm Only Cumin

Episode 213 | AIRDATE: November 3, 2023 | PREP TIME: 10 minutes | Makes one sandwich

I feel like it's not particularly easy for the average person to estimate how much a tablespoon is. It is at least true of the average McElroy brother. Though originally pitched by Justin during the season 5 wild magic collaboration, all three of the brothers signed off on adding one tablespoon of cumin to a sandwich as being "a lot, but not too much." Well, on November 3, in the year of our Lord 2023, I got to experience firsthand just how much cumin is in one tablespoon. (Spoiler alert: It's too much!)

I actually find it astounding that this sandwich rated higher than zero. It is only through a very specific set of dice rolls that this was made possible—literally everything other than the cumin was some sort of liquid, spread, or paste. The result was a bit like biting into kinetic sand between two slices of bread, but I fear the alternative (an abundance of loose and completely dry cumin) would have been worse (and possibly dangerous?).

I hope that this "recipe" stands solely as an interesting oddity or maybe a warning and that you don't actually make this sandwich. The shrimp cheese in a tube from Sweden is worth trying, but not like this (never like this). I also can't imagine that consuming that much cumin in one sitting is good for you. I did it so you don't have to!

INGREDIENTS

- 2 slices brioche bread
- Natural crunchy peanut butter
- Strawberry jam
- Shrimp mjukost
- 1 tablespoon* ground cumin
- Hot honey mustard

*Tablespoon is not a typo. I'm so sorry.

INSTRUCTIONS

1. Toast the slices of brioche and lay them side by side on a plate.

2. Spread peanut butter on one slice of the bread.

3. Spoon some strawberry jam on top of the peanut butter and spread it around until evenly coated.

4. Squeeze some shrimp mjukost from the tube onto the other slice of bread and spread it evenly with a knife.

5. Measure out the entire tablespoon of cumin and sprinkle it over the jam, making sure to evenly distribute it as much as possible (not that it will help).

6. Spoon out the hot honey mustard on top of the shrimp cheese and spread it with the back of the spoon until it creates an even layer.

7. Close the sandwich by placing the cheese and mustard slice of bread sauce side down on top of the rest of the sandwich.

8. Cut it in half diagonally and carefully eat. (Seriously—don't breathe in too sharply with this sandwich close to your mouth unless you want to know what it's like to breathe cumin.)

I have to believe there are probably still some unknown side effects to ingesting this much ground cumin in one sitting.

CURIOSITIES

Welcome traveler, to my treasure trove of oddities and wonders! Though most, if not all, of the sandwiches on Roll for Sandwich are strange in some way, these amazing specimens push the boundaries of concepts like "sandwich" and "edible" further than any before them. Feast your eyes (and perhaps *only* your eyes) on these incredible feats of deli daring!

6/10

The Beginning

Episode 1 | AIRDATE: April 12, 2022 | PREP TIME: 5 minutes | Makes one sandwich

The first-ever Roll for Sandwich episode resulted in what is still one of the most normal sandwiches of the show. I didn't have any wacky ingredients in the house when I began this journey, just a fun concept. I had no idea I would even be making a second episode, and now, you're reading my cookbook!

The dice decided to start me out easy. The rich pastrami was nicely cut by the acid in the pickles and mustard, and the soft seeded bread added some nice texture. All in all, a pretty tame combination, if a bit salty. The weirdest thing about this sandwich is probably its lack of cheese, which I do think it could have used. My process has changed so much over the years of doing this show, but the core of Roll for Sandwich, lunch decided by fate, has been here from the beginning.

Looking back on this episode, I laugh when I think about rating this sandwich a 6/10. Of course, I had no other randomly generated sandwiches to compare it to, but I still think 6 was a little harsh. These days, The Beginning would rate at least two full points higher, easily. There have been some real stinkers since then (and the worst offenders are included in this book if you dare to seek them out).

INGREDIENTS

- 2 slices of seeded bread
- 1½ ounces pastrami
- 6 dill pickle slices
- Salt and pepper
- Yellow mustard

INSTRUCTIONS

1. Lay the slices of seeded bread on a plate.

2. Lay the pastrami in an even layer on top of one of the slices of bread.

3. Add the pickles slices in an even layer on top of the pastrami.

4. Sprinkle salt and pepper over the pickles.

5. Drizzle yellow mustard over the pickles, or, if you prefer, on the other slice of bread.

6. Close the sandwich by putting the second slice of bread on top of the one with toppings. If you added mustard to the bread, place it mustard side down.

7. Enjoy *uncut* for the most accurate re-creation!

The first Roll for Sandwich episode created a classic sandwich (giving very little indication of the highs and lows to follow).

The Beginning 95

10/10

The Za-mbie

Episode 84 | **AIRDATE: October 19, 2022** | **PREP TIME: 20 minutes** | **Makes one sandwich**

This sandwich is a prime example of using what you have. It's in some ways more consistent with the original spirit of Roll for Sandwich than many of the others. These days, I often buy things specifically for the show, but the first episode included only what I had on hand. With this sandwich, we rolled two of the options specifically designed to help me use up leftover food (the "freezer ends" and "leftovers" rolls, respectively), so we really did use whatever was on hand!

I particularly like the leftovers roll because it makes me add things to the sandwiches that I never would have thought of. I try to be creative when adding ingredients to my lists, but the leftovers roll often goes beyond things I'd think of. This sandwich had an entire pizza slice, while other episodes have featured tacos and even an entire fast-food chain burger in the middle of a sandwich! Keeping a spot reserved for leftovers provides the opportunity to minimize food waste, keeps things interesting, and even sometimes ends up creating an unexpectedly tasty sandwich.

The Za-mbie is packed to the brim—the pizza, extra cheese, bacon, avocado . . . it's a lot! But, in this case, it's delicious. I'd just recommend enjoying this one sporadically, perhaps once in a harvest moon.

INGREDIENTS

- 2 slices challah bread, toasted
- 1 leftover slice of pizza
- 2 slices fontina cheese
- 2 ounces avocado
- ¼ cup cucumber
- 2 slices of precooked bacon
- 1 ounce Florida-style barbecue sauce

Tip
If you don't have challah available, use any bread you might have stored in your freezer—it's definitely within the spirit of this sandwich.

INSTRUCTIONS

1. Lay the challah slices out on a plate.

2. Reheat the pizza slice however you see fit. (My favorite method is on the stovetop in a hot pan covered with a lid—this crisps up the bottom and melts the cheese.) Once reheated, place the pizza slice on top of one of the slices of bread. (If you want to re-create my sandwich exactly, make sure your pizza has green pepper, mushroom, and green olive on top.)

3. Use a cheese slicer or knife to slice two sandwich-sized slices of fontina. Layer the slices of cheese on top of the pizza.

4. Peel and halve the avocado and remove the pit. Cut the avocado into slices, then add the slices in a layer on top of the cheese.

5. Cut about a 3" (7.6cm) segment from the cucumber and slice that longways into strips. Layer these strips on top of the avocado.

6. Prepare the bacon, then place the warmed bacon on top of the cucumber.

7. Drizzle the barbecue sauce onto the other slice of bread.

8. Close the sandwich by adding the top slice of bread sauce side down.

9. Cut the sandwich in half diagonally and enjoy!

> **Tip**
> I prefer to use precooked bacon for sandwiches—it is quick and easy to prepare in small batches.

Pizza in the middle of a sandwich has to be tried at least once!

9.5/10

Sandwichception

Episode 130 | AIRDATE: March 3, 2023 | PREP TIME: 20 minutes | Makes one sandwich

Sometimes, even when the sandwich takes a hard left turn into chaos, it's not enough to ruin it. In this case, that chaos took the form of a strawberry fruit snack, but fortunately, there was so much else going on that it got lost in the mix. Oh, did I mention this sandwich uses *two* grilled cheese sandwiches as bread? The fact that this wasn't even the most chaotic thing about this sandwich really demonstrates how this show can go sideways. In this case, though, it was a welcome departure from the norm.

For a sandwich made from two grilled cheese sandwiches, this was still an almost perfect execution by the dice. The pepperoni, giardiniera, and pesto took things into a spicy Italian, pizza-y direction that was really nice, and these flavors were strong enough to overpower a little bit of extra sugar.

Other than the obvious, the radish was the only outlier here. There was nothing wrong with its inclusion, but it didn't do enough to justify being there. If I were making the sandwich again purposefully, I'd nix the radish and Roll-Up, perhaps in favor of fresh or sun-dried tomato. I might even suggest modifying the preparation methods to also warm the entire sandwich rather than just the two exterior grilled cheese sandwiches. Feel free to experiment with this one, it has a lot of potential!

INGREDIENTS

- 4 slices buttered white bread
- 4 slices processed American cheese
- 2 ounces sliced pepperoni
- 1 slice Swiss cheese
- ¼ cup thinly sliced radish
- 2–3 ounces giardiniera
- 1 strawberry Fruit Roll-Up, or a suitable alternative, optional
- 2 ounces pesto

INSTRUCTIONS

1. Put the buttered bread slices on a hot skillet, butter side down.

2. To two of the slices of bread, add two slices each of the American cheese.

3. Take the two remaining slices of bread and flip them on top of the American cheese, creating two cheese sandwiches. Flip both sandwiches and continue to grill them until the cheese melts and the bread is browned but not burnt.

4. Once grilled, remove the sandwiches from the heat and place them next to each other on a plate.

5. On top of the grilled cheese sandwich that is acting as the "bottom bun," add the pepperoni slices in an even layer.

6. Add the Swiss cheese on top of the pepperoni.

7. Add the radish slices on top of the Swiss cheese in an even layer.

8. Add a few generous spoonfuls of giardiniera on top of the radish. For a less messy sandwich, first drain off some of the oil from each spoonful of giardiniera.

9. Optional: Unroll the Fruit Roll-Up and add it on top of the giardiniera. (Only do this step if you are going for an accurate reconstruction of the sandwich. It is better left off, truth be told.)

10. Spread the pesto on one side of the "top bun" grilled-cheese sandwich, then, pesto side down, place it on top of the Fruit Roll-up (or giardiniera if you wisely choose to forego the sweet intrusion).

11. Cut the sandwich in half diagonally and enjoy!

Try this sandwich with some of the modifications I've recommended in the introduction—I'd love this sandwich to have even more opportunities to shine!

6.3/10

The Fetch Quest

Episode 200 | AIRDATE: September 29, 2023 | PREP TIME: 20–120 minutes | Makes one sandwich

For the landmark 200th episode of Roll for Sandwich, I knew I had to do something special, and this sandwich was the result! The challenge was to use only ingredients from nearby fast-food restaurants and, for better or worse, that's what I did.

I rolled all my dice and, with the list in hand, I went online to chart the best course to visit six different fast-food restaurants back to back. With that done, I hopped in the car and set out on my mission. It took a little over an hour of driving and waiting in drive-thrus (and cost about $50 to create this single sandwich), but our quest was successful.

This is in no way a practical sandwich to make. Of course, there is the issue of value: Making odd requests like this at fast-food restaurants often leads to being overcharged because their systems can't really handle special accommodations. Freshness is also an issue. After about an hour of driving, the items that were collected at the beginning of the voyage were definitely cold by the time the final sandwich was assembled and eaten. If I had an entire team working on it, I could perhaps have timed things so that everything was at least a little fresher for the taste test, but, for now, this is a one-man show.

I can't really, in good conscience, recommend that you do this one. It works as a concept for a viral video stunt but, as a recipe, it does not. Save yourself both time and money and just get food from a single restaurant. Then again, I'm not your dad—do what you want.

INGREDIENTS

- 1 Tim Hortons Boston cream donut, or a suitable alternative
- 4 Wendy's spicy chicken nuggets, or a suitable alternative
- 1 slice McDonald's American cheese, or a suitable alternative
- 2 ounces KFC whole kernel corn, or a suitable alternative
- 1 ounce Qdoba pickled onions, or a suitable alternative
- 1 McDonald's baked apple pie, or a suitable alternative
- 2 ounces Culver's® Signature Sauce, or a suitable alternative

INSTRUCTIONS

1. Acquire the ingredients. I recommend plotting out your route ahead of time and traveling to each restaurant using the most efficient route to try to keep your ingredients as fresh as possible. This is most likely a lost cause. You've been warned.

2. Once you return home with several bags of fast food and feelings of moderate social embarrassment, begin assembling the sandwich.

3. With a bread knife, slice the donut in half, bun-style. Lay the two halves on a plate, cut side up.

4. Arrange the nuggets in an even layer on top of the bottom donut slice.

5. Place the slice of cheese on top of the nuggets.

6. Add a few spoonfuls of corn on top of the cheese. I recommend using a slotted spoon to avoid adding too much liquid to the sandwich.

7. Add a layer of pickled onions on top of the corn.

8. Use a knife to carefully butterfly open the apple pie. Use a spoon to scoop out the filling. Realize this is futile and just add whatever bits of the pie that you can to the sandwich.

9. Spread the signature sauce on the cut side of the top donut bun.

10. Add the top donut bun, sauce side down, to the rest of the sandwich.

11. Cut the sandwich in half and let the weight and disappointment of what you just spent the last two hours doing sink in.

12. Take a bite, I guess.

This is a true oddball of a sandwich. It wouldn't be easy to replicate, but maybe you can create your own version at a single local fast-food restaurant?

The Fetch Quest

8.5/10

Tom

Episode 256 | AIRDATE: March 4, 2024 | PREP TIME: 60 minutes | Makes one little guy

Tom lived his life the way he died, slowly going soggy, and, though he was only with us for a short time, his memory lives on. When I received the prompt of "Humanize It" from the McElroy Brothers (of *The Adventure Zone* podcast) during our 2023 collab, I had no idea what to do with it at first.

They wanted me to transform the sandwich of the day into a "little guy" with arms, legs, and a backstory. It was one of the more conceptual prompts from them for sure. Finally, about six months later, when almost all other options for the collaboration had already been rolled, we finally landed on "Humanize It"—and Tom was the result.

I did what anyone in my position would do. I gathered up some doll clothes and a few items my infant had recently outgrown, and I constructed a body to affix the sandwich "head" to, thus creating Tom. Through the magic of an emotional music montage, I formed a close bond with Tom, sharing with him the beauties of our local area, complete with a visit to the park. As Tom's inner joy rose to match his outer temperature (suboptimal for eating), I knew his time was drawing near.

I became the sandwich Abraham to Tom's Isaac and offered him upon the altar of my cutting board. Alas, no benevolent God intervened. Then I ate Tom. He was pretty good, if a little warm.

INGREDIENTS

- 2 slices tomato basil bread
- 3 ounces corned beef brisket, sliced
- 2 slices Swiss cheese
- ¼ cup cucumber
- 2 ounces giardiniera
- 1 ounce Tubby's® Famous Dressing, or a suitable alternative

INSTRUCTIONS

1. Toast the tomato basil bread slices and lay them out on a plate.
2. Place the corned beef brisket on the bottom slice of bread in an even layer.
3. Place the slices of Swiss cheese on top of the corned beef in an even layer.
4. Layer the thinly sliced cucumber on top of the Swiss cheese.
5. Spread the giardiniera on top of the cucumber.
6. Drizzle with the dressing.
7. Construct a body and face for your little sandwich boy. I used a plastic soda bottle and baby and doll clothes to create his body and legs and used a small piece of note paper for his face. There is no exact science to this step, it's more about quickly using what you have to make your sandwich into a little guy.
8. Give your little sandwich guy a good time during his short existence on earth. I took mine on an outing to the park!
9. Usher your sandwich offspring into the great beyond by cutting it in half diagonally.
10. Like Saturn devouring his son, consume the flesh of your little sandwich friend.
11. Make a therapy appointment.

R.I.P., Tom. I barely knew you.

9.4/10

The Frozen Pizza

Episode 120 | AIRDATE: February 10, 2023 | PREP TIME: 5 minutes | Makes one sandwich

When I listed ice cream as an option on the roll sheets, I 100 percent expected it to be an instant failure when it was rolled. The fact that it became the pivotal ingredient in one of the most memorable sandwiches to date was a pleasant surprise and one of the big reasons that I make this show in the first place. You truly never know what's going to work until you taste it!

One of the reasons that this sandwich works is its simplicity. I know, I'm seeing those raised eyebrows—the sandwich may indeed have ice cream on it, but relatively speaking, it's simple as far as the flavor pairings go, or maybe "balanced" is a better way to put it. The vanilla ice cream and queso fresco are both pretty mild, the former adding mostly a fun texture, the cool temperature, and a little sweetness.

The Frozen Pizza is one of the most unique sandwich experiences I've had, on or off the show. The novelty treat "ice cream sandwiches" that you can find in almost every American grocery store (ice cream in between cookies or graham crackers) is always sweet. It's a dessert. The Frozen Pizza is nearly an entirely savory and sour experience—one that I urge you to try if you are up for something different!

INGREDIENTS

- 2 slices wheat bread
- 12–16 slices pizza-style pepperoni (if using sandwich-style pepperoni, you will only need 2–4 slices)
- 2 ounces queso fresco
- 7 ounces vanilla ice cream
- 1½ tablespoons Colman's Mint Sauce, or a suitable alternative

INSTRUCTIONS

1. Lay two slices of wheat bread on a plate.
2. Cover one of the slices entirely with the pepperoni.
3. Cut the queso fresco into slices and layer them on top of the pepperoni in an even layer.
4. Cut a slice of ice cream roughly the same size as the slices of bread.
5. Place the ice cream slice on top of the queso fresco.
6. With a spoon, drizzle the mint sauce over the ice cream so that it is evenly distributed over the entire sandwich.
7. Close the sandwich by adding the second slice of bread on top.
8. Cut the sandwich in half diagonally, and enjoy immediately (before it melts).

Tip

The easiest way to cut slices of ice cream is to buy the ice cream in a square box carton, one that allows you to fold down the sides to reveal the entire brick of ice cream. It's easy to just slice some off.

Alternatively, you can scoop the ice cream out onto a cutting board and use a second cutting board to press it flat. I'd recommend greasing or flouring both cutting boards to keep the ice cream from sticking.

This was a savory and sour ice cream sandwich—bizarre but balanced (and tasty).

The Frozen Pizza

7.2/10

The Brittle Lily

Episode 312 | AIRDATE: September 4, 2024 | PREP TIME: 10 minutes | Makes one sandwich

Sometimes an item gets featured on the show that seems doomed to fail but then ends up surprising me. Peanut brittle has been on a few sandwiches so far and has been intriguing each time. I am a big proponent of having something crunchy on a sandwich, as the difference in textures makes things interesting. Peanut is a versatile flavor—even though we often associate it with sweets in the US, it is a salty, savory legume that pairs well with many different foods. Obviously, in the case of peanut brittle, it is accompanied by sugar, but not so much that it will push every sandwich over the edge into being a dessert.

Peanut brittle was not the death knell for this sandwich that I thought it would have been—the sandwich still rated a 7.2/10.

There are plenty of elements here that balance out the extra sugar, including the vinegary barbecue sauce. It might have been even better with a little bit of a spicier sauce to lean into the Thai peanut sauce vibes. There is a combination out there where peanut brittle on a sandwich earns a 10/10. Maybe someday we will discover it together!

INGREDIENTS

- 1 slice pumpernickel bread
- 1 slice Italian bread
- 3 slices olive loaf
- 2 slices Swiss cheese
- ¼ cup thinly sliced green pepper
- 1–2 large iceberg lettuce leaves
- 1 ounce peanut brittle
- Carolina-style barbecue sauce

INSTRUCTIONS

1. Place one slice of pumpernickel bread and one slice of Italian bread side by side on a plate.

2. Evenly layer the slices of olive loaf on top of the slice of Italian bread.

3. Add the cheese on top of the olive loaf in an even layer.

4. Arrange the slices of green pepper on top of the cheese in an even layer.

5. Arrange the lettuce leaves on top of the green pepper in an even layer.

6. Arrange pieces of the peanut brittle into an even layer on top of the lettuce.

7. Spread the Carolina-style barbecue sauce on the slice of pumpernickel bread.

8. Close the sandwich by putting the slice of pumpernickel, sauce side down, onto the rest of the sandwich.

9. Cut the sandwich in half diagonally and enjoy!

An odd mix of ingredients sometimes almost lands, then doesn't quite make it to true greatness.

The Brittle Lily 107

9.1/10

The Beverly Hillbilly

Episode 297 | AIRDATE: June 28, 2024 | PREP TIME: 20 minutes | Makes one sandwich

Ever since Roll for Sandwich took off, I have been constantly on the lookout for new things to feature on the show. It has allowed me to try new things, for good or ill, and has taught me so much about food. There are times, however, when the dice put me in a position that feels a bit . . . philistine.

This sandwich has a rather large portion of morel mushrooms on it. Morels are almost entirely foraged rather than cultivated. It is possible to grow them, but it takes three to five years of up-front investment without any guarantee of success. They only grow in the wild for a relatively short season, for a few weeks in the spring and in very specific conditions. All this scarcity makes them expensive (the fact that they're delicious also helps). I put them in a sandwich with bologna and frozen French toast. I'm not proud of it.

The comedy of the juxtaposition of expensive gourmet mushrooms with cheap meat notorious for being made of the "rejected bits" and premade, ready-in-two-minutes toaster fodder is the only redeeming factor. That, and the fact that this Jed Clampett of a sandwich actually tasted pretty good, gives me . . . mixed feelings.

INGREDIENTS

- 2 slices frozen French toast
- 2 slices bologna
- 2 slices provolone cheese
- ¼ cup chopped green onion
- 1 cup morel mushrooms
- Salted butter
- Korean barbecue sauce

INSTRUCTIONS

1. Toast two slices of frozen French toast according to the package instructions and set them side by side on a plate.

2. Place two slices of bologna onto one of the slices of French toast.

3. Arrange the green onion in an even layer on top of the bologna.

4. Carefully wash the morel mushrooms. Sauté them whole on medium to medium-high heat in a frying pan with salted butter. Cook for 7–10 minutes, stirring occasionally.

5. Once the mushrooms are cooked, remove them from the heat and place them in an even layer on the sandwich.

6. On top of the mushrooms, add an even layer of provolone cheese and melt it with a kitchen torch.

7. Drizzle the Korean barbecue sauce onto the other slice of French toast.

8. Close the sandwich by placing the sauced piece of French toast, sauce side down, onto the rest of the sandwich.

9. Cut it in half diagonally and enjoy!

The absurd mix of the deluxe and the discount—and it tasted great.

2.9/10

The Shadow of a Trout

Episode 319 | AIRDATE: September 20, 2024 | PREP TIME: 10 minutes | Makes one sandwich

I'm a fairly adventurous eater; you have to be to make a show like this. I make a conscious effort to try new things all the time and to not make any prejudgments. Even still, I have my preferences. I tend not to enjoy fish if it tastes fishy. It's weird because I also love sushi (although I do usually stick with tuna, which doesn't bother me). Tinned fish has consistently put me off. Some of the worst sandwiches I've had on the show have had things like sardines in them. In the spirit of being adventurous, however, I just keep bringing tinned seafood back to the show. Eventually, maybe, I'll find one that I really like. As a certified disliker of tinned fish, this tinned trout wasn't actually all that bad. I think with the right pairings, I might even call it good. Marshmallows and salad cream are definitely not the right pairings. Still, it's impressive that a tinned-fish sandwich wasn't an immediate zero!

INGREDIENTS

- 1 slice pumpernickel bread
- 1 slice Hawaiian bread
- One 3.2-ounce tin of smoked trout with lemon and cracked pepper
- 2 slices extra sharp cheddar
- ½ of a Roma tomato, sliced
- 2 tablespoons marshmallow bits
- Salad cream

INSTRUCTIONS

1. Place one piece of pumpernickel bread and one piece of Hawaiian bread on a plate side by side.

2. Open the tin of trout and scoop the fish out with a fork onto the slice of Hawaiian bread. Discard the excess oil from the tin.

3. Add the extra sharp cheddar on top of the trout.

4. Arrange the tomato slices on top of the cheese in an even layer.

5. Sprinkle marshmallow bits over the tomatoes. The moisture from the tomatoes will help them stick. Oh boy.

6. Spread salad cream on the slice of pumpernickel bread.

7. Close the sandwich by placing the pumpernickel sauce side down onto the rest of the sandwich.

8. Cut the sandwich in half diagonally and there you go. Now you get to eat it. Good for you.

Tip

If you want to be fully accurate in re-creating my sandwich from the show, the Hawaiian bread should be frozen when you put it on the plate. Don't worry, it will thaw quickly.

It says something that this sandwich featuring tinned fish didn't score a zero. Not a lot, but there's something there.

6/10

Chopped & Screwed

Episode 271 | **AIRDATE: April 19, 2024** | **PREP TIME: 10 minutes** | **Makes one "sandwich"**

This is another episode of Roll for Sandwich that really tests the limits of what we can call a sandwich. You would probably be much better off just making a mortadella and cheddar sandwich than attempting to re-create this one. Removing the sliced bread and replacing it with loose croutons made eating this one experientially much more akin to nachos than sandwich (and far less enjoyable than either). Croutons are significantly inferior to tortilla chips in their ability to carry ingredients.

The typical sandwich-eating experience is just about as perfect as it can get—two slices of bread acts as a great vehicle for so many foods. Sandwiches are easy to eat with little to no mess—even sandwiches like tuna salad. This "sandwich" resembles a tuna salad sandwich in form, except for the crucial element of replacing the easy-to-hold bread slices with individual croutons. Frankly, it's a recipe for disaster, and an entirely unpleasant eating experience.

Tactile torture aside, it didn't end up tasting too bad, though it was a bit of a shame to have to do that to such quality ingredients. The mortadella is rich and salty and goes nicely with the sharp cheese. The whiskey element of the cheese is nicer when enjoyed by itself—you can appreciate the flavor more when it doesn't have to battle other flavors for supremacy. Overall, it's a fairly decent sandwich that was docked several points for the mode in which it was presented. Do with that what you will.

INGREDIENTS

- 2 ounces seasoned croutons
- 2 ounces mortadella with pistachios
- 1½ ounces Irish whiskey cheddar
- 1 medium sour garlic pickle
- 1 ounce Japanese mayo

INSTRUCTIONS

1. Arrange one ounce of the seasoned croutons on a plate to resemble a slice of bread. Set aside the rest of the croutons for later use.

2. Chop and mix the mortadella, cheese, and pickle together. I prefer to use a concave cutting board and Alaskan ulu knife, but a regular knife and cutting board will also work.

3. Place the chopped ingredients in a bowl and add the Japanese mayo. Mix everything until it's well incorporated.

4. Spoon the chopped mixture onto the croutons you set out earlier, spreading it in an even layer.

5. Add the remaining croutons that were set aside earlier on top in an even layer, closing the "sandwich."

6. Eat with your hands, creating tiny crouton-enclosed salad sandwiches for each bite.

Just think of it as "sandwich nachos," or, better yet, just *don't* think about it.

7/10

Cretaceous Cookie Crumble

Episode 168 | **Airdate: June 30, 2023** | **Prep time: 20 minutes** | **Makes one sandwich**

This sandwich seems to ask the question, "What would a five-year-old make if they were given unrestricted access to the kitchen?" Either that or, "What if a dispensary could write recipes?" This sandwich starts with two big cookies—and not just any cookies, two of those loaded cookies from a gourmet bakeshop that have become so popular in the last decade that are absolutely covered in fruity cereal.

But wait, there's more. Let's add chicken nuggets. Wait, no! Dino nuggets! Yep. The dice were 100 percent possessed by a small child that day. Then, we toss on not one, but two different sliced fruits and finish it off with a spice blend and mayo. The sandwich sprinkle spice blend is delicious, but it was the most out-of-place element of the whole sandwich—even more than the mayo, which actually pairs okay with fruit. If you've ever had a Waldorf salad, you know what I mean.

Though things kind of work with this one, it's nothing to write home about. It's a little overwhelming but doesn't have much substance . . . kind of like a five-year-old.

INGREDIENTS

- 2 fruit cereal cookies
- 5 dinosaur-shaped chicken nuggets
- 2 slices provolone cheese
- ¼ Granny Smith apple, sliced
- 2 small apricots, sliced
- Sandwich sprinkle spice blend
- Japanese mayo

Tip

You can make your own sandwich sprinkle. Simply mix salt, garlic powder, black pepper, dried basil, marjoram, rosemary, oregano, and thyme to your tastes.

INSTRUCTIONS

1. Place two large fruit cereal cookies side by side on a plate, topping side up.

2. Preheat the oven to 425°F (218°C). Place the nuggets on a baking sheet and cook them for 10–12 minutes, flipping the nuggets halfway through.

3. Arrange the nuggets on top of one of the cookies in an even layer.

4. Place the provolone on top of the nuggets in an even layer.

5. Arrange the apple slices on top of the cheese in an even layer.

6. Add the sliced apricots in a thin layer on top of the apple.

7. Sprinkle the spice blend over the apricots.

8. Drizzle with the Japanese mayo.

9. Close the sandwich by adding the other cookie, topping side down, to the rest of the sandwich.

10. Cut the sandwich in half and enjoy!

You may not be ready for this sandwich yet... But your kids are gonna love it!

Cretaceous Cookie Crumble

5.1/10

The Ferryman's Fee

Episode 191 | AIRDATE: September 8, 2023 | PREP TIME: 15 minutes | Makes one sandwich

The Ferryman's Fee is such a strange collision of cultures. Living in West Michigan, I have an easier time than most accessing traditional Dutch ingredients. I can find really nice Gouda, for example, and, yes, salty black licorice. I've never worn clogs, but I have been to the annual Tulip Time Festival in Holland, Michigan, several times. If the people at the Dutch village knew what I was buying their cheese and candy for, though, they'd likely be hesitant to sell it to me again.

The dice demand chaos, however, so when they demand a salty black licorice sincronizada, that's what we give them! A sincronizada is a Mexican sandwich made on tortillas usually containing cheese and ham, which is toasted to melt the cheese. It's different from a quesadilla, which is typically one tortilla folded over with cheese inside. I had no idea of the distinction until some commenters pointed it out on this very video. I learn so much from the Roll for Sandwich community!

This sandwich was surprisingly okay. Licorice has a little more flexibility than other confections because of the anise flavor, especially this licorice, which isn't super sweet but rather borders on savory. It's a decent candidate for a candy that would actually work on a sandwich with meat and cheese. The biggest issue I foresaw was the texture since the coins are extremely chewy. On a cold sandwich, they would have been the nail in the coffin for sure, but since they were heated, they softened up quite a bit and were actually palatable. There may be an ideal pairing for them out there somewhere, but for now, they rest at a 5.1/10, which, frankly, is probably higher than they deserve.

INGREDIENTS

- 2 large flour tortillas
- 4 slices deli turkey
- 2 slices provolone cheese
- ½ cup snow peas in the pods
- 9 double salt black licorice coins
- Stonewall Kitchen Maine Maple Champagne Mustard, or a suitable alternative

INSTRUCTIONS

1. Place a large flour tortilla in a cold, nonstick pan.

2. Place the turkey slices on top of the bottom tortilla in an even layer. Try to cover as much of the tortilla as possible.

3. Split the provolone cheese into pieces and distribute them evenly on top of the turkey. (You could really use more cheese, but that day I only had two slices left.)

4. Arrange the snow peas evenly on top of the cheese.

5. Add the licorice coins, evenly spacing them on top of the layer of peas.

6. Drizzle with the Maple Champagne Mustard.

7. Top with the other tortilla, then cook in the pan on medium heat for a few minutes, flipping halfway through. Your goal is to melt the cheese without burning the tortilla.

8. Cut the sandwich in half and enjoy. When you bite in, watch out for the licorice—it will be hot!

They weren't the best addition to a sandwich, but warmed up, the licorice coins were at least easy enough to eat.

6.7/10

The Pickle Priest

Episode 339 | AIRDATE: November 13, 2024 | PREP TIME: 10 minutes | Makes one sandwich

Sandwiches like this make it very difficult for some people not to think the show is scripted. If you've played TTRPGs for any length of time, you know that the dice have a sense of humor. It is entirely possible for you to critically miss a level one goblin five times in a row, even using a different die for every roll—strange things happen all the time! To me, this is one of the funniest episodes of the show ever, through no effort on my part. It's pure comedy that we started with pickle and pretty much stayed pickle the whole time. (The double-buttering was also pure comedic gold!)

Taste-wise, it's not a bad sandwich. Based on taste alone, it could be rated quite a bit higher. Unfortunately, a jumbo pickle is just not a great vehicle for a sandwich. I'm all for alternatives to bread. I understand the reasoning behind opting to build your sandwich on some type of vegetable—less carbs, gluten-free, the list goes on—and I don't disparage anyone who prefers that in the slightest. Just know that there are better sandwich vessels than a pickle. Lettuce, for example, works great—it's big and you can roll it like a tortilla. A pickle, however, requires you to scoop out half of it to even have a chance at being viable. A pickle is also inherently . . . wet. That wetness translates to a very messy sandwich that isn't worth all the work you'd have to go through just to avoid bread.

INGREDIENTS

- 1 jumbo dill pickle
- ½ ounce salted butter
- 8–10 pizza-style pepperoni slices
- 1 slice Gouda cheese
- ¼ cup cucumber, sliced
- ⅛ cup sour garlic pickles, sliced
- Pickle juice
- Japanese mayo

INSTRUCTIONS

1. Slice the jumbo dill pickle in half, longways, and place the two halves face up on a plate.

2. With a spoon or a melon baller, remove the seeds and core portion of the pickle, hollowing out an area for the sandwich fillings.

3. Spread butter on both halves of the pickle. This is easier said than done since the pickle is wet and the butter will not want to stick to it. I guess "spread" isn't really the right word . . . "scoop little bits of butter into both halves of the pickle" is probably more accurate.

4. On one half of the pickle, arrange the pepperoni slices in an even layer.

5. Tear or cut the slice of Gouda in half and place the two halves on top of the pepperoni so that the whole pickle-half is covered.

6. Thinly slice the cucumber and arrange the slices on top of the cheese in an even layer, then do the same with the sour garlic pickles.

7. Fill a spray bottle with pickle juice and spritz both halves of the sandwich, because there wasn't enough pickle already.

8. Drizzle Japanese mayo on top of the sour garlic pickles.

9. Close the sandwich by placing the other pickle-half, hollowed side down, onto the rest of the sandwich.

10. Cut the sandwich in half and enjoy!

Pickles are great, they just weren't made to house a sandwich.

Undiscovered Treasures

Through over 400 sandwiches, I have lain upon the altar of fate for my lunch. I have had only a small amount of control over the outcome each time, and that has been my chosen lot. Each time I learned. Each time I gained knowledge. This is my time to shine—or at least to experiment! These sandwiches are recipes I've created exclusively for this book using all that I have learned in making this show. I've gained a ton of XP. There's no dice-rolling involved—it's solely my leveled-up knowledge skill at work! I hope you enjoy them all!

The Roc Salad Wrap

PREP TIME: 10 minutes | Makes one sandwich

There is a small but vocal contingent of Roll for Sandwich viewers who are adamantly "anti-wrap." If something isn't between two slices of bread, to them it is not a sandwich and has no business on the show. I like to take a more inclusive approach to sandwiches. For certain ingredients, a wrap is just a better vehicle—and I still very much consider it a sandwich.

The Roc Salad Wrap was inspired by a salad that I had once, and as such, has many small bits that would not stay easily contained betwixt bread. A tortilla, however, delivers them beautifully. I have made this one several times since dreaming it up for inclusion in this book, and each time it gets better. I love the contrast of crunchy pistachios and pomegranate arils against the creamy chicken salad, and then the tartness of the pomegranate and goat cheese and the acid of the mustard with the sweetness of the honey and richness of the mayo is a delight. Truly one for the books!

INGREDIENTS

- One 10" (25.4cm) flour tortilla
- ½ cup chicken salad (an actual roc may be hard to come by . . . it's also much more dangerous than the chickens)
- ½ cup chopped romaine lettuce
- ¼ cup pomegranate arils
- ¼ cup goat cheese crumbles
- 1 tablespoon salted, shelled pistachios
- Salt and pepper
- Brown mustard
- Honey

INSTRUCTIONS

1. Heat a nonstick frying pan on the stovetop over low heat.

2. Once the pan is warm, add the tortilla. Warm the tortilla, flipping it occasionally, until it becomes malleable, then remove it from the heat and set it on a plate.

3. Place scoops of chicken salad in a line down the center of the tortilla, leaving room on both sides to fold it into a wrap.

4. Add the lettuce in a line on top of the chicken salad.

5. Add the pomegranate arils, goat cheese crumbles, and pistachios, being sure to distribute them evenly.

6. Sprinkle everything with the salt and pepper.

7. Lay one or two stripes of brown mustard along the length of the wrap.

8. Drizzle on the honey.

9. Tuck in the ends of the tortilla and roll everything into a wrap. Secure it with toothpicks.

10. Cut the wrap (which is very much a sandwich) in half and enjoy!

Sometimes wraps are the best way to get a particularly delicious combo of ingredients into your mouth! (And not on your shirt.)

The P.B.P.

PREP TIME: 5 minutes | Makes one sandwich

My goal with these exclusive sandwiches was to keep them accessible while still having some of that trademark RFS chaos. There are several sandwiches in this book that include multiple off-the-wall ingredients, and the likelihood that the average person is going to take the time and effort to search all of them out to re-create a sandwich that they aren't even sure they will enjoy is honestly pretty low. I intend for the rarities here at the end of the book to be sandwiches that most people can realistically reproduce. It goes to show that you don't have to be outrageous every time you make a sandwich, but you can still think a little bit outside the box sometimes to surprise yourself with delicious results!

INGREDIENTS

- 2 slices white bread
- ¼ cup crunchy peanut butter
- 2 tablespoons piccalilli

INSTRUCTIONS

1. Toast the pieces of white bread and set them side by side on a plate.

2. On one slice, spread the crunchy peanut butter. On the other slice, spread the piccalilli.

3. Close the sandwich by putting the peanut butter and piccalilli sides together.

4. Cut the sandwich in half diagonally and enjoy!

This sandwich is perfectly designed to challenge your preconceived notions of peanut butter. Who knows? Maybe one day it'll be as popular as the PB&J!

The Bologna Buzz

Prep time: 10 minutes | Makes one sandwich

Bologna and hot dogs get a bad rap. True, they aren't the healthiest meats for you, and they are best eaten in moderation, but there is no denying that they are tasty! I also appreciate them because they use parts of the animal that many find to be less desirable. I am all about the reduction of food waste, and if we are going to raise animals for consumption, then we should absolutely make sure that none of their sacrifice goes to waste.

I wanted to make a sandwich that highlighted bologna's strengths. It's fatty, rich, and salty, but it also pairs well with both sweet and savory flavors and especially well with acidic flavors like peppers. This simple fried bologna sandwich takes the basic bologna flavor and elevates it with the frying, bringing out more richness via that good old Maillard reaction (the chemical process that transforms certain amino acids and sugars into complex, more flavorful molecules—long story short: heat make food taste good). The honey and mustard bring the sweet and acid. This is an easy masterpiece to throw together without much advance planning, so go make it!

INGREDIENTS

- 2 slices sourdough bread
- 4 slices bologna
- 2 slices Muenster cheese
- 2 tablespoons honey
- 1 tablespoon yellow mustard
- Salted butter

INSTRUCTIONS

1. Heat a pan on the stovetop over medium heat.

2. Cut a slit in each slice of bologna and add them to the pan. Fry them until they're browned, flipping when necessary.

3. Once fried, remove the bologna from the pan, but do not turn off the heat. Butter two slices of sourdough bread and add them to the pan butter side down.

4. Place the bologna on top of one of the slices of bread in the pan.

5. On top of the bologna, layer two slices of Muenster cheese.

6. Add a small amount of water to the pan and cover it. Cook it until the cheese melts.

7. In a small dish or ramekin, combine the honey and yellow mustard, then spread the mixture on the empty slice of bread.

8. Close the sandwich by flipping the top piece of bread over onto the rest of the sandwich, sauce side down. Remove the sandwich from the heat.

9. Cut the sandwich in half diagonally and enjoy!

Some combinations are meant to be. Fried bologna and cheese? Honey and mustard? No question—we've got a winner.

The Strawberry Fairy

PREP TIME: 25–35 minutes | **Makes one sandwich**

There have been many episodes in which an odd sweet ingredient has completely ruined an otherwise good sandwich. This has happened enough times for people to ask on a fairly regular basis if I've ever gotten a *completely* sweet sandwich. That hasn't happened on the show yet (The Elephant in the Room is the closest we've come), but the question has had me thinking for a while about what an excellent sweet sandwich would look like.

The Strawberry Fairy is my experimental attempt at creating that dessert sandwich for this book. It draws inspiration from a few existing recipes from outside American culture. The first is fairy bread. Fairy bread is an Australian dessert made with bread, butter, and sprinkles (specifically nonpareils, or, as they call them, hundreds and thousands). It's a common treat at children's birthday parties (and I've made a sandwich or two using fairy bread on the show—just nothing as cohesive as this).

The second bit of inspiration for this sandwich is the Japanese "ichigo sando" (literally "strawberry sandwich"), which consists of crustless milk bread, fresh whipped cream, and strawberries. Cream and fruit sandwiches are popular in Japan and can be found in many shops and convenience stores.

I wanted this sandwich to be accessible to the average American, so instead of using Japanese milk bread, it uses plain white bread. The flavors are similar to strawberry shortcake, if a little less sweet, and the crunch of the nonpareils adds a nice little surprise. The next time you're in the mood for a light, sweet snack, give this a try!

INGREDIENTS

- 2 slices white bread
- Salted butter
- Nonpareils
- ½ cup whipped topping
- ¼ cup sliced strawberries

INSTRUCTIONS

1. Cut the crust off of two pieces of soft white bread and butter them. Be careful not to shred the soft bread. If the butter is too firm, try whipping it.

2. Sprinkle both slices of bread with the nonpareils until they are each covered in an even layer.

3. Place a piece of cling film on a cutting board and place one slice of bread in the center. Set the other piece of bread aside for now.

4. Add half the whipped topping to the slice of bread.

5. Add a layer of strawberry slices on top of the whipped topping.

6. Cover the strawberries with the rest of the whipped topping.

7. Add the other slice of bread, nonpareil side down, on top of the rest of the sandwich.

8. Carefully wrap the sandwich in the cling film and place it in the freezer for 20 to 30 minutes to allow everything to set.

9. Remove the sandwich from the freezer, carefully unwrap it, and place it on a cutting board.

10. Use a bread knife to carefully cut the sandwich in half diagonally. Enjoy!

Fairy Bread + Ichigo Sando = A delicious sweet sandwich the entire Pacific can be proud of.

The Goodberry

PREP TIME: 35 minutes | Makes one sandwich

I've had quite a few creations come close to being pure "breakfast sandwiches" in the American sense, but none have been absolute standouts in the series. So, when I was tasked with coming up with some original recipes for this book, I knew one of them had to be a breakfast sandwich.

There are some things you can get away with in a breakfast sandwich that you can't as easily for other meals. My favorite is probably combining sweet and savory. Breakfast is often a meal that is eaten quickly. You're not typically sitting down for an entire entrée with sides. You are looking for something to give you energy for the morning that can get you to lunch without being so filling that you just want to go back to sleep. The portions are usually smaller, so your sandwich can usually be richer.

The Goodberry combines a sweet, fruity, French toast–like bread with a slathering of jam and the salty savoriness of bacon and eggs. The Crème de Brie® pulls it all together with richness that's cut perfectly by the tartness of the strawberry (and even better by the Tajín.) It's a small, succulent breakfast treat that will start your day off on a decadent foot!

INGREDIENTS

- 2 slices strawberry swirl bread
- Salted butter
- 2 eggs
- Milk
- 3 strips precooked bacon
- 1 ounce alouette® Crème de Brie, or a suitable alternative
- Strawberry jam
- Salt and pepper
- Tajín, optional

INSTRUCTIONS

1. Butter the slices of strawberry swirl bread and lay them side by side on a plate. Set them aside.

2. Crack the eggs into a bowl and add a splash of milk. Whisk them or use an eggbeater until the yolks and whites are thoroughly mixed and you have a nice froth on top.

3. Heat a pan over medium heat and add the egg mixture. Keep the eggs moving, scrambling them until they are soft and still a little wet. Transfer the eggs from the pan into a bowl or dish and set them aside.

4. Place the slices of bacon on a paper towel and microwave them for 30 seconds on high or until properly heated (the exact time will depend on your microwave). Remove them from the microwave and dab any grease off the top with another paper towel. Set the bacon aside.

5. On the stovetop, warm a medium frying pan over medium heat. Place both slices of bread butter side down into the pan next to each other.

6. On one slice of bread, spread a layer of the Crème de Brie. Spoon scrambled eggs over it in an even layer.

7. Season the eggs with salt and pepper. Optional: Add the Tajín if you prefer less sweetness.

8. Cut each bacon strip in half and layer them on top of the seasoned eggs so that the bacon covers the entire slice of bread.

9. On the other slice of bread, spread a generous layer of strawberry jam.

10. Close the sandwich by flipping the jammed slice of bread over onto the rest of the sandwich, jam side down. Continue cooking the sandwich until the bread is golden brown, being careful not to let it burn.

11. Once the sandwich is cooked, remove it from the pan with a spatula and place it on a cutting board.

12. Secure it with toothpicks and cut it in half diagonally. Enjoy!

Tip
If you can't find strawberry swirl bread, I recommend using cinnamon raisin or brioche instead.

This is an upgraded breakfast sandwich perfect for parties, brunches, special occasions, birthdays . . . or, honestly, every day.

Your Own Adventure: Roll for Sandwich at Home

It's time to gather your ingredients and your favorite dice and roll. In this section, you'll find instructions, tips, and roll sheets to help you kick off your own Roll for Sandwich adventure. It's time to get rolling, get building, and have fun! And remember—waste nothing! Every combination deserves to be rated and devoured (if not always enjoyed).

HOW TO ROLL FOR SANDWICH

So, you think you have what it takes to be a culinary adventurer? Are you truly ready to delve deep into the dungeon of randomized ingredients and toppings-based traps? I believe in you, adventurer, but before you go, heed my instructions . . .

1. Assemble the basic tools for RFS. You will need:
   - TTRPG dice
   - Roll sheets, see pages 134–139
   - A dice tower, dice tray, or bowl
   - A writing implement

2. Fill in your roll sheets with the food items you have available or plan to have available. You can buy ingredients specifically for your adventure or just use what you have on hand. Put breads (or anything else you could put sandwich ingredients in) on the Bread list; meats, vegan mains, or anything else that could work as the focal point of a sandwich on the Mains list; cheeses on the Cheese list; vegetables and fruits on the Roughage list (I even include mushrooms in this category, even though it's a fungus); and sauces on the Sauce list. The Wild Magic list is a catchall category for everything else, and the place where you can really put anything—spices, bacon strips, candy, pretty much anything you can imagine that doesn't really fit on one of the other sheets. Don't be afraid to get creative—and remember, when compiling your lists, be mindful of waste.

3. Starting with your bread sheet, roll the type of die shown on the roll sheet (1D6) and record your result. Fate has just decided the first ingredient for your recipe!

Tip
When a number precedes the "D," it means you should roll that many dice. For example, "2D6" means you need to roll two six-sided dice.

4. Continue through each roll sheet, rolling the corresponding die or dice as indicated on the sheet (see the tip above). Record each result as you roll, and, once finished, you will have the recipe for your sandwich.

5. Now that you have your randomly generated sandwich recipe, build your sandwich using the required ingredients, and enjoy!

CHOOSING ITEMS FOR THE ROLL SHEETS

There are two approaches you can use when filling out the ingredient lists on your roll sheets. You can also combine the two approaches.

The first approach is to use only items you already have in your house/kitchen. This is a great option if you are alone, are spontaneous, or want to challenge yourself to use up the ingredients you have lying around. It is okay to reduce the number of items listed on a Roll Sheet, just leave the higher spots blank and roll a smaller die. For example, if you only have 10 sauces instead of 20, just fill in slots 1 through 10 on the sauce list and roll a D10 instead of a D20. Just

make sure to keep the number of items on your sheet consistent with one of the existing dice sizes, or you may end up rolling an invalid option. If that does happen, though, it's okay—just roll again!

The second approach is to go shopping with Roll for Sandwich in mind. This is the best approach if you're hosting a Roll for Sandwich party where multiple people will be rolling their own sandwiches. Purchasing every possible menu item for Roll for Sandwich (6 different breads, 12 vegetables, 20 sauces, etc.) means buying a *lot* of food. I would carefully consider the ingredients and amount you're buying for any such event.

For popular, "normal" options like white bread and cheddar cheese, go ahead and buy larger portions as needed, especially if you are confident you will use any leftovers. If you are buying a "weird" or challenging item to make things fun and interesting, consider buying it in a small amount (especially if it is something you don't think anyone would willingly eat as leftovers). It's far better to run out of the "weird" item than to throw a large portion of it away after the party.

SOURCING INTERESTING INGREDIENTS

Here are a few tips to keep in mind if you want to add ingredients outside of your normal repertoire to your Roll for Sandwich experience.

The international section of your grocery store is a great place to start. Don't worry about not knowing what things are—start small and be adventurous! Grab something that looks interesting off the shelf. If you have time, do a little research on your phone right there in the aisle.

If you've already thoroughly explored the international section of the grocery store, a trip to a specialty shop might be in order. There are many Asian and Mexican markets near where I live, and I love exploring them and finding cultural foods I haven't been exposed to before. Just make sure you are doing it with a spirit of adventure, curiosity, and respect. Even when an item might not be to your liking, remember that it isn't part of a "gross-out challenge." This is food that real, everyday people eat, enjoy, and were raised on. Treat it with respect.

Another way to make things interesting is to think outside the box and get creative with familiar foods. Waffles, graham crackers, nori seaweed sheets, and even lettuce can all be options on the "bread" list. It doesn't have to be strictly bread, as long as it fulfills the same purpose within the sandwich structure. If you're playing with kids, take a stroll down the candy aisle. It's always a hoot when someone gets gummy worms on their sandwich, and you *know* the leftovers won't go to waste.

Whatever you decide, have fun and keep an open mind. Remember, these are all just suggestions. Roll for Sandwich, just like any other TTRPG, isn't about following every directive to a T, it's about having fun and telling a good story—"rule of cool" forever! Now, let's get rolling!

BREAD - 1D6

1 _____   **4** _____

2 _____   **5** _____

3 _____   **6** _____

CHEESE – 1D6 [6]

1 _____ **4** _____

2 _____ **5** _____

3 _____ **6** _____

ROLL FOR SANDWICH

MAIN – 1D12

1 _____

2 _____

3 _____

4 _____

5 _____

6 _____

7 _____

8 _____

9 _____

10 _____

11 Roll Again

12 Butter + Roll Again

ROUGHAGE – 2D12

1 _____

2 _____

3 _____

4 _____

5 _____

6 _____

7 _____

8 _____

9 _____

10 _____

11 None

12 Roll 2D12 Again

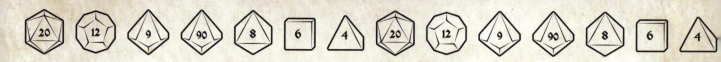

SAUCE – 1D20

1 _____
2 _____
3 _____
4 _____
5 _____
6 _____
7 _____
8 _____
9 _____
10 _____

11 _____
12 _____
13 _____
14 _____
15 _____
16 _____
17 _____
18 _____
19 _____
20 Dealer's Choice

ROLL FOR SANDWICH

WILD MAGIC – 1D20

1. _____
2. _____
3. _____
4. _____
5. _____
6. _____
7. _____
8. _____
9. _____
10. _____
11. _____
12. _____
13. _____
14. _____
15. _____
16. _____
17. _____
18. _____
19. _____
20. Dealer's Choice

FAQs

- **It's your show, why do you put bad stuff on the list at all?**
  I think it is more entertaining to watch when there is an element of risk involved—it's higher drama. The "will he succeed, or crash and burn?" of it all is good storytelling.

- **What is the thing you roll dice in called?**
  It's called a dice tower. The first one I used in the series (which I've been using the longest), I purchased from LootEverything on Etsy. Josh, who made the tower, now works for a company called Talon & Claw. You can actually purchase a Roll for Sandwich–branded dice tower on their website! Visit *https://shoptalonclaw.com/pages/roll-for-sandwich*.

- **How often do you eat sandwiches when you're not filming? Do you ever get sick of them?**
  Honestly, I probably eat too many sandwiches! They are one of my favorite foods, and I don't really ever get tired of them. I might get tired of a certain combo, but that's part of what's so great about sandwiches—the possibilities are pretty much endless!

- **Do you really finish every sandwich?**
  Yes. I don't like to waste food. Also, I feel like it's more entertaining or exciting if the stakes are real. The only time I don't finish the sandwiches is when we do a live show, and that's just because we are making 6 to 7 sandwiches in 2 hours or so (and that's definitely too much). I'm very clear about this at the live shows, however.

- **Has there ever been a sandwich that you just couldn't finish?**
  At the time of writing, no. I have come close to throwing in the towel a couple of times, but I haven't had to yet.

- **Has a sandwich creation ever gotten you sick?**
  It depends on what you mean by sick. Have I ever thrown up? No. Have I had heartburn or indigestion? Yes.

- **How big is your fridge/freezer/kitchen? How do you always have so much food? How do you keep all your ingredients fresh?**
  I actually live in a very small house with a tiny kitchen. It is definitely not the ideal location for producing a cooking show, but my family and I love our house. I currently just have a regular refrigerator and a small chest freezer in the garage. I do have an overflowing "RFS" cabinet with all the sauces and shelf-stable stuff that people have sent me for the show. That became necessary very early on.

  I work really hard to avoid food waste. I keep my ingredients fresh by limiting what I keep on hand. You may notice that my bread often comes from my freezer, or that I use a lot of pickled ingredients (since they last a long time). For fresh ingredients, I prioritize what to use up and do my best to keep track of what I have.

- **Are you allergic to anything?**
  No foods that I know of.

RECIPE CONVERSIONS

Use the following conversion chart for liquids and larger dry ingredients. Since the masses of some dry ingredients (pastes, ground herbs, etc.) will be different depending on how they are manufactured, you should research the correct conversion for the exact ingredient you are using.

½ tablespoon = 7.5mL	¼ cup = 60mL	1 ounce = 28g
1 tablespoon = 15mL	½ cup = 120mL	2 ounces = 56g
2 tablespoons = 30mL	1 cup = 240mL	6 ounces = 170g
⅛ cup = 30mL	½ ounce = 14g	½ pound = 227g

■ **Is there anything you refuse to try or put on the show?**

There are things I have not put on the show yet because I know when I do, they will likely be bad. I'm kind of saving them for when I need something big. I also try to make sure I'm always being respectful and not making a spectacle of other cultures' foods, so sometimes I'm waiting for the right setting or collab with someone more knowledgeable than me. I am always considering new things to add to the list, even if they scare me. Currently, the only line I've drawn is edible insects, and that's less of a taste thing and more of a "generally being skeeved out by insects" thing. That's not to say that it will never happen. It just might have to be for charity or something.

■ **Do you have a culinary background? You seem so knowledgeable.**

Well, thank you! I work hard on my research for the show. The truth is that I don't really have a culinary background. Food has been an interest of mine since I was a little kid. My grandmother was always cooking and always had cooking shows on at her house. I grew up watching her work and being exposed to a ton of new foods through her. She taught me how to be an adventurous eater, and I've run with her lesson. I've worked some low-level food service jobs but never anything with any actual cooking involved. In my early twenties, I was a big fan of Chef Andrew Zimmern's *Bizarre Foods* show, where he would travel to different countries and try all kinds of exotic food. I think this helped shape the way that I look at food, especially food from cultures outside my own. I'm always learning more every day, and that's part of what makes this show so fun. I may sound like a pro, but often the things I'm sharing with you today I learned just yesterday!

■ **How do you come up with ideas for things to put on the show?**

I just keep my eyes open constantly. I'm a foodie, so if I'm watching something and a new food I've not heard of comes across my screen, I look into it and add it to my wish list for the show. If I'm traveling, I make an effort to visit shops and places where I'll find ingredients I wouldn't normally encounter. My community also sends things to my PO Box or through my online wish lists.

If you want to send me an ingredient for the show, you can!
Please make sure it is shelf stable (no fresh meat, cheese, bread, produce,
or anything that needs refrigeration prior to opening).

You can send your packages to:
Adventures in Aardia
PO Box 150993
1765 3 MILE RD NE, GRAND RAPIDS, MI 49505-9998

Index

Aberdeen buttery, Pure Dead Brilliant on, 30–31
The Abomination, 74–75
advantage/disadvantage, defined, 9
All Taffy, No Laughy, 78–79
avocado, sandwiches with, 12–13, 52–53, 72–73, 96–97

bacon and Canadian bacon
    about: precooked bacon, 16
    The Jurassic Pork, 16–17
    The Merle, 20–21
    The Slawful Good, 34–35
The Bad Buddy, 86–87
beans, on Beanhamut, 82–83
beef. *See also* pastrami
    All Taffy, No Laughy, 78–79
    The Comfortably Numb, 38–39
    Risk It for the Brisket, 18–19
    Sweet Summer Pie, 58–59
    Tom, 102–3
The Beginning, 94–95
berries
    The Goodberry, 130–31
    I'm Only Cumin, 90–91
    Sandwichception, 98–99
    The Strawberry Fairy, 128–29
The Beverly Hillbilly, 108–9
black pudding, on Pure Dead Brilliant, 30–31
bologna
    The Beverly Hillbilly, 108–9
    The Bologna Buzz, 126–27
    The Crabomination, 76–77
    How the Nog Stoll Christmas, 64–65
    The Jurassic Pork, 16–17
    The Toast Balone-y, 40–41
bread, roll sheet, 134
bread, types of. *See* specific sandwiches
buttery, Aberdeen, 30–31

Canadian bacon, The Merle, 20–21
candy and cookies, sandwiches with. *See also* chocolate
    The Bad Buddy, 86–87
    The Brittle Lily, 106–7
    Cretaceous Cookie Crumble, 114–15
    The Ferryman's Fee, 116–17
    The H.O.A., 68–69
    The Nasty Patty, 80–81
    The Nightmare Before Christmas, 66–67
cantrip, defined, 9
cheese, sandwiches featuring. *See also* pizza
    about: cheese roll sheet, 135; Peppadew cheddar, 32

The Cheese Blessing, 26–27
Curd to the Wise, 44–45
The Elephant in the Room, 50–51
Sandwich a la King, 42–43
Sandwichception, 98–99
The Swiss Near Miss, 48–49
The Cheese Blessing, 26–27
chicken
    The Abomination, 74–75
    Cretaceous Cookie Crumble, 114–15
    Curd to the Wise, 44–45
    The Demi Delhi-catessen, 22–23
    The Fetch Quest, 100–101
    The Roc Salad Wrap, 122–23
    The Rotten Soldier, 28–29
    The Slawful Good, 34–35
chocolate
    The Cold Day in Shell, 60–61
    The Elephant in the Room, 50–51
    How the Nog Stoll Christmas, 64–65
Chopped & Screwed, 112–13
chorizo, on The Descent into Avernus, 88–89
Christmas. *See* festival of seasons
The Cold Day in Shell, 60–61
coleslaw, on The Slawful Good, 34–35
The Comfortably Numb, 38–39
conversions, recipe, 141
cookies. *See* candy and cookies, sandwiches with
The Crabomination, 76–77
cream donut, The Fetch Quest on, 100–101
Cretaceous Cookie Crumble, 114–15
critical hits, 10–35
    about: defined, 9; overview of sandwiches, 10
    The Cheese Blessing, 26–27
    The Crunch Squad, 24–25
    The Demi Delhi-catessen, 22–23
    The 42, 12–13
    Ginger Dreams, 14–15
    The Jurassic Pork, 16–17
    The Merle, 20–21
    The Peppadew® Pig, 32–33
    Pure Dead Brilliant, 30–31
    Risk It for the Brisket, 18–19
    The Rotten Soldier, 28–29
    The Slawful Good, 34–35
croutons, on Chopped & Screwed, 112–13
The Crunch Squad, 24–25
Curd to the Wise, 44–45
curiosities, 92–119
    about: overview of sandwiches, 92
    The Beginning, 94–95
    The Beverly Hillbilly, 108–9
    The Brittle Lily, 106–7

Chopped & Screwed, 112–13
Cretaceous Cookie Crumble, 114–15
The Ferryman's Fee, 116–17
The Fetch Quest, 100–101
The Frozen Pizza, 104–5
The Pickle Priest, 118–19
Sandwichception, 98–99
The Shadow of a Trout, 110–11
Tom, 102–3
The Za-mbie, 96–97
cusp of greatness, 36–53
    about: overview of sandwiches, 36
    The Comfortably Numb, 38–39
    Curd to the Wise, 44–45
    Dim Sum Pair-O-Dice, 46–47
    The Elephant in the Room, 50–51
    Sandwich a la King, 42–43
    The Swiss Near Miss, 48–49
    Taste of the Wild, 52–53
    The Toast Balone-y, 40–41

D&D, defined, 9
Deck the Halls, 84–85
The Demi Delhi-catessen, 22–23
The Descent into Avernus, 88–89
Dim Sum Pair-O-Dice, 46–47
disadvantage/advantage, defined, 9
DM/GM, defined, 9
D20, D6, etc., defined, 9

eggs
    The Goodberry, 130–31
    How the Nog Stoll Christmas, 64–65
    Sandwich a la King, 42–43
The Elephant in the Room, 50–51
epic failures, 70–91
    The Abomination, 74–75
    about: disclaimer/warning about, 70; overview of sandwiches, 70
    All Taffy, No Laughy, 78–79
    The Bad Buddy, 86–87
    Beanhamut, 82–83
    The Crabomination, 76–77
    Deck the Halls, 84–85
    The Descent into Avernus, 88–89
    The Failed Stealth Check, 72–73
    I'm Only Cumin, 90–91
    The Nasty Patty, 80–81

The Failed Stealth Check, 72–73
failures. *See* epic failures
FAQs, 140–41
The Ferryman's Fee, 116–17
festival of seasons, 54–69. *See also* Deck the Halls
    about: overview of sandwiches, 54

142 ROLL FOR SANDWICH COOKBOOK for Gaming Enthusiasts and Adventurous Eaters

The Cold Day in Shell, 60–61
The Heart Attack, 56–57
The H.O.A., 68–69
How the Nog Stoll Christmas, 64–65
The Nightmare Before Christmas, 66–67
The PureBREAD, 62–63
Sweet Summer Pie, 58–59
fiddleheads, on Taste of the Wild, 52–53
fish and seafood
  The Crabomination, 76–77
  The Failed Stealth Check, 72–73
  The H.O.A., 68–69
  I'm Only Cumin, 90–91
  The Nasty Patty, 80–81
  The Shadow of a Trout, 110–11
flower petals, on Curd to the Wise, 44–45
The 42, 12–13
The Frozen Pizza, 104–5

ginger
  about: pickled, 14
  Ginger Dreams, 14–15
  The H.O.A. (gingerbread house kit), 68–69
The Goodberry, 130–31

ham, on The Swiss Near Miss, 48–49
The Heart Attack, 56–57
The H.O.A., 68–69
hot dogs, on The Abomination, 74–75
How the Nog Stoll Christmas, 64–65

ice cream, The Frozen Pizza, 104–5
I'm Only Cumin, 90–91
ingredients. See recipes; Roll for Sandwich at home; *specific main ingredients*
ingredients, sourcing, 133

jackfruit, on The Nightmare Before Christmas on, 66–67
The Jurassic Pork, 16–17

mac and cheese, on Sandwich a la King, 42–43
McElroy Brothers, 20, 24, 60, 90, 102
The Merle, 20–21
mimic, defined, 9
mortadella, on Chopped & Screwed, 112–13
mushrooms, on The Beverly Hillbilly, 108–9

The Nasty Patty, 80–81
Nat 20, defined, 9
The Nightmare Before Christmas, 66–67

olive loaf, on The Brittle Lily, 106–7

pastrami
  The Beginning, 94–95
  The Heart Attack, 56–57
The P.B.P., 124–25
peanut brittle, on The Brittle Lily, 106–7
peanut butter
  The 42, 12–13
  I'm Only Cumin, 90–91
  The P.B.P., 124–25
  The Rotten Soldier, 28–29
The Peppadew® Pig, 32–33
pepperoni
  The Frozen Pizza, 104–5
  The Pickle Priest, 118–19
  Sandwichception, 98–99
  The Slawful Good, 34–35
  The Toast Balone-y, 40–41
The Pickle Priest, 118–19
pickled ginger, 14
pickles
  masala, 22
  Old Bay, 20
  The Pickle Priest, 118–19
pizza
  The Frozen Pizza, 104–5
  The Za-mbie, 96–97
pork. See also bacon and Canadian bacon; bologna; salami
  The Cold Day in Shell, 60–61
  The Crunch Squad, 24–25
  Dim Sum Pair-O-Dice, 46–47
  The Jurassic Pork (with SPAM), 16–17
  The Peppadew® Pig, 32–33
  The Swiss Near Miss (with ham), 48–49
Pure Dead Brilliant, 30–31
The PureBREAD, 62–63

questions (FAQs), 140–41

recipes. See also Roll for Sandwich at home; *specific main ingredients*; *specific recipe categories* (critical hits; curiosities; cusp of greatness; epic failures; festival of seasons; undiscovered treasures)
  about: this book and, 6–7
  conversions chart, 141
  FAQs, 140–41
  Roll for Sandwich story and, 6, 7–8
  why sandwiches, 8
reindeer pâté, on Deck the Halls, 84–85
Risk It for the Brisket, 18–19
The Roc Salad Wrap, 122–23
Roll for Sandwich at home, 132–41. See also recipes; *specific main ingredients*
  choosing items for roll sheets, 132–33
  FAQs, 140–41
  how to Roll for Sandwich, 132

roll sheets (bread; cheese; main; roughage, sauce), 134–38
  sourcing interesting ingredients, 133
Roll for Sandwich (video series), 6
roll sheets. See Roll for Sandwich at home
The Rotten Soldier, 28–29
RPG/TTRPG, defined, 9

salad wrap, 122–23
salami. See also pepperoni
  The Bad Buddy, 86–87
  Chopped & Screwed, 112–13
  Ginger Dreams, 14–15
  The H.O.A., 68–69
  Taste of the Wild, 52–53
Sandwich a la King, 42–43
sandwich recipes. See recipes; *specific main ingredients*
Sandwichception, 98–99
sauces
  boom boom sauce, 42
  copycat Big Mac sauce, 52
  roll sheet, 138
sausage, on The Descent into Avernus, 88–89
seafood. See fish and seafood
seasons. See festival of seasons
The Shadow of a Trout, 110–11
The Slawful Good, 34–35
Spam, on The Jurassic Pork, 16–17
spell slot, defined, 9
The Strawberry Fairy, 128–29
Sweet Summer Pie, 58–59
sweets. See candy and cookies, sandwiches with; chocolate; ice cream
The Swiss Near Miss, 48–49

tabletop gaming terms, 9
taffy, on All Taffy, No Laughy, 78–79
Taste of the Wild, 52–53
The Toast Balone-y, 40–41
Tom, 102–3
Trout, The Shadow of a, 110–11
TTRPG/RPG, defined, 9
turkey
  The Ferryman's Fee, 116–17
  The PureBREAD, 62–63

undiscovered treasures, 120–31
  about: overview of sandwiches, 120
  The Bologna Buzz, 126–27
  The Goodberry, 130–31
  The P.B.P., 124–25
  The Roc Salad Wrap, 122–23
  The Strawberry Fairy, 128–29

The Za-mbie, 96–97

About the Author

Jacob A. Pauwels is a writer and internet content creator based in Grand Rapids, Michigan, where he lives with his wife, two children, and miniature poodle.

He enjoys Star Wars®, board games, playing TTRPGs, building LEGO®, and reading fantasy and sci-fi novels.

He has a bachelor's degree in television production from Ferris State University, and his Tiktok channel, *@adventuresinaardia*, has over 2.4 million followers.

For more from Jacob, Adventures in Aardia, and Roll for Sandwich, visit *www.rollforsandwich.com* and subscribe to his newsletter at *www.knightsofsandwich.com*.